Small Gardens
Violet Biddle

Small Gardens
And How to Make the Most of Them

by
Violet Purton Biddle

SPINEBILL PRESS

© Spinebill Press 2020

All rights reserved. Apart from any fair dealing for the purposes of private study, research, criticism or review permitted under the Australian Copyright Act 1968, no part may be stored or reproduced by any process without prior permission. Enquiries should be made to the publisher.

Spinebill Press
Katoomba NSW, Australia
spinebillpress.com

 A catalogue record for this book is available from the National Library of Australia

ISBN 978 0 6485315 2 4

Design and typography by Michel Streich
Typeset in Caslon

Contents

The General Arrangement of the Garden 7
Lawns, Paths, Beds, and Border 13
On the Duty of Making Experiments 19
Some Neglected but Handsome Plants 23
The Conservatory and Greenhouse 30
The Tool Shed and Summer House 36
Roses for Amateurs 44
Enemies of the Garden 58
The Rockery 62
Trees, Shrubs, and How to Treat Them 77
The Ins and Outs of Gardening 89
The Profitable Portion 95
Annuals and Biennials 103
Window Boxes 108
Table Decoration 114
The Propagation of Plants 123
The Management of Room Plants 128
Various Hints 137
Calendar 143
Terms Used by Gardeners 156

CHAPTER I

The General Arrangement of the Garden

What to go in for, and what to avoid ~ Brick walls ~ Trees, their advantages and disadvantages, etc.

It is imperative that a small garden, such as one generally finds attached to suburban or small houses, should be made the very most of. Frequently, however, its owners seem to think that to attempt to grow anything in such a little plot of ground is a veritable waste of time and money, as nothing ever comes of it. The aim of this book is to show that even the tiniest piece of land can be made pretty and even profitable, if due attention be given it.

Well begun is half done

To begin with, it is well to remember that the tenant of a small garden should not endeavour to represent every feature he sees in large grounds; the poverty-stricken shrubbery and pond just about large enough for a nice bath, are too often seen, and only call forth ridicule. Some landscape gardeners have even objected to the presence of a lawn, where the space at disposal is very limited indeed, but to my mind a little turf is always advisable, for it not only entices people into the fresh air for a game, but forms a good foil for flowering plants, and above all looks so well during the winter.

A long narrow garden is always easier to deal with than a square plot of land, the range of vision not being 'brought up short', as it were. It is well to take heed of this fact where there is any choice in the matter. Good brick walls are a great help in gardening, though alas! in these hurried days they are becoming much rarer, the wooden fence being run up so quickly, and at far less expense.

As regards the walks, it is better to have one path wide enough for two people abreast than several unsociably narrow ones. Each path should lead somewhere, to the summer house, or a gate, for instance: otherwise it looks inconsequent.

Besides the flower garden proper, a nursery for making experiments, sowing seeds, and striking cuttings, should find a place, if possible; a rubbish heap is invaluable, too, where all decayed vegetable refuse, road scraping, soapsuds, etc., should be thrown. In autumn, all the leaves the gardener sweeps up should be placed near by, both heaps being frequently turned over to allow of the noxious gas escaping, and to assist decomposition. The rubbish corner should be at the furthest extremity of the garden, though it need not be unsightly if a screen is placed around it. Privet is certainly the quickest growing shrub for that purpose, but, as it is so common, other shrubs, such as *Pyrus japonica*, *Arbutus*, barberry, and pyracantha, may be used.

The joys of a greenhouse

If there is no greenhouse, try to obtain one; it is such an infinite delight all through the dark months of the year, and this without any great cost for fuel. A Rippingille oil stove, with one four inch wick, will suffice to keep the frost out of a structure measuring 16×10, if a lean-to (that is, attached to a dwelling house). Even this expense may be avoided where it is built against a kitchen wall, though, if the wall happened to face north, only ferns and just a few flowers would thrive. But even these would form a great interest, especially to invalids, who often find their greatest pleasure in pottering about under their 'little bit of glass'.

A vexed question

The vexed question of lopping one's neighbours' trees is sure to crop up sooner or later. However much detriment the trees may be doing, by preventing the free access of sun and air, tenants should know that the law only justifies them in cutting down those branches which actually overhang their own domains. This being the case, it is often the best 'to grin and bear it', and lop the trees as little as possible, for we must acknowledge that the fine form of a tree is always spoilt when interfered with to any great extent. If the border would, in any case be shady, so much the better; it will only require a little more attention in the matter of watering, etc. After all, shade from the hot summer sun is absolutely necessary if we would enjoy a garden, therefore it is always well to hesitate over an act which takes but a few minutes to do, but may need years to repair. Where the trees overhang a good south or west wall the matter is more serious; it is then advisable to cut back as far as possible, for roses, peach trees, and, indeed, most climbers resent the constant drip they are obliged to endure in wet weather. A list of plants which do well under trees in various aspects is given in another chapter.

Breaking up

As the eye wearies of the straight piece of lawn with gravel path and border surrounding it, where practicable the ground should be broken up a bit.

Some wide trelliswork, painted dark green, with an archway on either side, helps to do this, and lends a pleasant sense of mystery to what might otherwise be a prosaic garden. It should be covered with all manner of creepers, such as clematis, jasmine, roses in variety, and some of the hardy annuals. Very tender plants should not be put on a trellis, as it does not by any means take the place of a wall, being more draughty than the open ground, though such things as the ceanothus will often live through several winters, and bloom beautifully every summer in such a spot, till an unusually hard frost kills them outright. Mulching, however, of which more anon (see Glossary), materially aids in preserving them.

In gardening it is the little things that tell. A mere trifle often makes the difference between failure and success. People will hardly believe, for instance, how important it is that certain plants should only receive soft water, and continue giving the water laid on by the company when all the time gallons and gallons of precious rain from heaven are running to waste. It is only a question of a tank to preserve it, which should be in an unobtrusive situation, though easily get-at-able. Where alpines are concerned, rainwater should be the only beverage, and this reminds me that a rockery on which to grow these gems of other countries is not such an impossibility in a town garden as might be thought by their scarcity.

How not to do it

The rockery, as seen in most gardens, both public and private, is too often an example of 'how not to do it'. A heterogeneous mass of clinkers, planted here and there with ivy, and exposed to the full force of sun and wind, is not to be named in the same breath with those at Kew, for instance. Of course, these are not made with bricks at all, but of soft grey stone, rather difficult to obtain by amateurs. Nevertheless, the shape and general characteristics may be copied; indeed, a day every now and then spent in the Royal Gardens at Kew or in any other well planned gardens, is a liberal education in such matters, and a great help in laying out a garden to good effect, though, naturally, everything must be considerably modified.

CHAPTER 2

Lawn, Paths, Beds, and Border

How to keep a lawn level ~ Paths, how to lay them ~ Beds and bedding ~ The new style versus the old ~ Flower borders and their backgrounds ~ Improvement of the soil.

The autocrat of the garden

We have spoken of the general arrangement of the suburban garden, and must now proceed to particularize. First as to the lawn: It might often be described as a thing invented to keep the journeyman gardener in constant work, for where that individual only comes for a day or even half a day each week (on which basis this book is written) he generally seems to occupy his time in rolling, mowing, and sweeping the grass. An endeavour should a made to curtail this lengthy business, if it can be done without hurting his very sensitive feelings. When a boot boy is kept, he can be set to roll the grass before and after it is mown, and also assist in the tidying up, thus giving the man leisure to attend to other matters. Where tennis or more especially croquet is played, great care should be taken to keep the turf level; inequalities can always be remedied in the winter or early spring. Fine soil should be scattered over each depression where these are only slight, and a little seed sown about March; but when the turf is very uneven it is a better plan to lift it, fill up underneath with soil, and re-lay, rolling well so that it may settle down properly. To keep a lawn even constant rolling is most necessary. Even when the lawn is smooth, it is as well to sow some seed in the spring of every year, for there are sure to be weeds to eradicate, and this is apt to leave bare patches which mar the beauty of any lawn. During hot, dry summers, water must be regularly applied or the grass will wither and perhaps die out altogether. Grassy slopes especially should be looked after, as they are the first to show signs of distress. Where there is no hose, a 'spreader' will be found a most useful adjunct to a water can, and is quite inexpensive. The knives of a mowing machine should not be set too low in warm weather, as close cutting of grass is often responsible for it turning brown.

The paths of a garden can be composed of several substances, gravel possibly being the best, as it is so easily renewed and kept in order. In cottage gardens delightful pebble walks with an edging of tiles can be sometimes seen, but unless plants having a mossy or cushion-like growth are allowed to fall over the tiles, this arrangement is rather stiff. When laying gravel down, see that it is of a 'binding' quality, and laid fairly thick, as this method is economical in the long run, because it can be easily turned. The paths must be kept clear of weeds, and, except in the wild portion, free also of moss, a difficult thing where the growth of trees is very rank. Picking up the path constantly with a rake and scattering common salt over it, is one way of keeping moss down. It is important that the centre of a path be higher than the sides, so that it should dry quickly after rain.

Beds and bedding

As regards the beds in the garden, these are usually all on the lawn, though a long raised bed with a path on either side looks extremely well if filled with flowers, and can be easily got at on dewy mornings without wetting the feet. Fantastic shapes are not advisable, unless carpet bedding is the style aimed at. Rose trees look best in round or oblong beds, and do not lend themselves to filling up stars, though a crescent-shaped bed suits the low growing kinds very well. As a rule only one or two different kinds of flowers should be used in the same bed, and if a good display of blossom is required these must be frequently changed. Cuttings a year old make the best bedding plants in a general way, for, though the quantity of bloom may not be quite so great, the habit is more bushy, the individual flower far finer, and the period of blossoming greatly prolonged. It has been found that many of the old-fashioned flowers bloom much better if they also are divided and new soil added. This is particularly noticeable in such flowers as delphiniums, campanulas, and japonica anemones. Once every two or three years, however, is often enough for these hardy denizens of our gardens.

Making the most of the land

A new style of bedding has cropped up lately, or rather a lesson that Nature has always been teaching us has at last been taken to heart, for the idea is really as old as the hills. Two plants flowering at different seasons are placed together where formerly each would have had a separate piece of ground; thus, a tall, autumn phlox will be seen rearing its panicles of flowers from a carpet of aubrietia, alyssum, or forget-me-not, which all flower in spring. In this way each foot of ground has something to interest us at all seasons of the year. Lilies have been planted amongst rhododendrons and azaleas for some time past, and now the system has been extended. When once we have made up our minds to have no bare soil, various schemes will present themselves to us. Bulbs can be treated so, to the great improvement of the garden, as when they grow out of some hardy herbaceous plant, their dying leaves which present such an untidy appearance are nearly hidden. This double system of planting is especially necessary in beds which are in full view of the house, as these must never look empty.

Wanted – an eye for colour

Borders are not so much trouble in this way, as, if the wall or fence at the back is well covered with a succession of flowering shrubs, this makes a very good background, and, as every artist knows, that is half the battle. The colours, however, must be carefully chosen, so that the plants in front blend with the creepers on the wall. The inconsistency of people in this matter is very noticeable, for they will mix shades in their borders which they would not dream of allowing on their dinner tables. Who has not had his teeth set on edge by the sight of a pinkish-mauve everlasting pea in juxtaposition with a flaming red geranium! it is repeated every year in scores of gardens, to the great offence of every artistic eye. Colours that quarrel so violently with each other should never be visible from the same point of view, but kept rigorously apart.

It is important that the soil of the border be of fairly good quality; if the staple be poor and rocky, plenty of loam must be incorporated with a small proportion of manure. On the other hand, if it is heavy, cold, and clayey, sand must be added to make it porous, and thus improve the drainage. Where the soil is not improved, some trouble should be taken to choose only those plants which will do really well in the particular soil the garden possesses.

CHAPTER 3

On the Duty of Making Experiments

Description of a small yet lovely garden ~ Colour schemes ~ The spring dell ~ A novel way of growing flowers ~ Variety in flower gardens.

'Be original!' is a motto that every amateur gardener should adopt. Far too few experiments are made by the average owner of a garden; he jogs along on the same old lines, without a thought of the delightful opportunities he misses. Each garden, however small, should possess an individuality of its own – some feature that stamps it as out of the common run.

I remember seeing a tiny strip in a large town quite fairy-like in its loveliness, and it has always been a lesson to me on what enthusiasm can do. The old lady to whom it belonged was not rich, but an ardent lover of all that is beautiful in nature and art; moreover, she did nearly all the work herself. Though it was situated amid smoke and dirt, it almost invariably looked bright and pretty, reminding one somehow, from its quaintness, of the 'days of long ago', for there were no geraniums, no calceolarias, no lobelias, and not a single Portugal laurel in the whole place. Gardeners of the red, white, and blue school, if any read this book, will open their eyes at all this, and wonder, maybe, how a proper garden could manage to exist without these indispensable plants. But then it was not a proper garden in their sense of the term; paths were winding instead of straight, flowers grew so well, and bloomed so abundantly that they even ran into the walks occasionally, and, what was yet more reprehensible, there was not a shadow of a box edging to restrain their mad flight! Roses and jasmine threw their long flower-laden shoots over the arches in wild luxuriance, and were a pretty sight, as viewed from the seat hidden in a bower near by.

There was a small fernery, too, containing some of the choicest specimens that can be grown in this country. Altogether it was a most charming little garden, and gave infinite pleasure to the owner and her friends; indeed, I for one have often been much less pleased with formal ground of several acres in extent, though the latter might cost a mint of money to keep up.

Experiments in the way of colour schemes are most interesting, and should appeal to ladies, who may gain ideas for their costumes from the blending of shades in their garden, or vice versa. Here a word of warning will not be out of place; do not rely too much on the coloured descriptions in the catalogues, for, as they are usually drawn up by men, they are frequently inaccurate; so many men are partially colour blind, and will describe a crushed strawberry as a carmine! Frequently a flower will change its colour, however, when in different soil and position, even in the same district.

The dell at Chertsey

A novel way of growing plants is to open up a spring dell. I wonder if any of my readers have ever seen the one on St. Ann's Hill, Chertsey? I will try to picture it here. A large basin is scooped out of the hill, and on the slopes of this basin are grown masses of rhododendrons and azaleas. Round the rim at the top is some light rustic fencing, partially covered with climbing plants, and there was also a narrow bridge of the same material. This dell could not be copied in very small gardens, because it should be so placed as to come upon one rather in the way of a surprise, but where there are any corners not quite in view of all the windows, a little ingenuity will make a lovely thing of it. The shrubs used need not be identical; less expensive plants may be grown in just the same way. Those on the slope of the dell will do best; the plants for the bottom must be carefully chosen, as, of course, they will get much moisture and little sun. Wallflowers would run to leaf in that position; and so, I am afraid, would forget-me-not; daisies (double ones) would revel there, however, particularly if the soil were made fairly rich; they are extremely reasonable in price, and easily obtained. Bluebells, wood anemones, doronicums, hepaticas, narcissus, snowdrops, all like such a situation, but perhaps the queen of them all is *dicentra spectabilis*, or 'lady's locket', as it is sometimes called; it has pink drooping racemes and finely cut foliage, and is generally found under glass, though it is never seen to such advantage as when well grown out of doors. This dell is the very place for it, as, when out in the open ground, rough winds injure its precocious blooms. The hardy cyclamen would do admirably, too, but these must be planted on the slope of the dell, as they need perfect drainage. In summer it should be a mass of filmy ferns, foxgloves, and hardy orchids; the best of the orchids is *cypripedium spectabile*, and it should be planted in peat and leaf mould, and in such a way that it is fairly dry in winter and well watered in summer. Experiments in the way of growing uncommon plants are always interesting; in the next chapter, therefore, I will mention a few unreasonably neglected plants, including some novelties which I can personally testify to as well worth obtaining.

CHAPTER 4

Some Neglected but Handsome Plants

The sweet old columbine ~ Bocconia cordata *at Hampton Court* ~ *Campanulas as continuous bloomers* ~ *The heavenly larkspurs* ~ *Christmas roses* ~ *The tall and brilliant lobelias* ~ *The Chinese lantern plants* ~ *Tufted pansies.*

We will begin alphabetically, therefore I will first say a few words regarding the pink-flowered *Anemone japonica*. Though the white variety (*alba*) is to be seen in every garden, the older kind is not grown half enough; perhaps this is owing to the peculiar pinkish shade of the petals, a colour that will harmonize with few others, and might be termed aesthetic; it should be grown in a large clump by itself or mixed with white; it flowers at the same time as *A. j. alba*, and equally approves of a rich and rather heavy soil, and also likes a shady place. Both kinds spread rapidly.

Aquilegias, or columbines, are most elegant plants, generally left to the cottage garden, though their delicate beauty fits them for the best positions; they do well on borders, and generally flower about the end of May; in a light soil they seed freely, and spring up all round the parent plant. Asters, the botanical name for Michaelmas daisies, are beautiful flowers for a small garden if the right sort are chosen; those that take up a great deal of room should be discarded where space is an object, and such kinds as *Aquilegias amellus bessaribicus*, planted instead; this is perhaps the finest of the genus, and is first rate for cutting. It is only two feet high, of neat habit, and bears large, bright mauve flowers with golden centres very freely, from the beginning of August right into October. *A. ericoides* is another one of neat habit, and is only half a foot taller than the last; it bears long sprays, covered the whole way up the stem with tiny white flowers and mossy foliage. Some of the *novi-belgii* asters are also very good and easy to grow. One of the most effective and beautiful plants in the summer months is *Bocconia cordata*; it has delicate, heart-shaped foliage of a clear apple-green, silvered beneath, and creamy flower spikes which measure from three to five feet in height; though so tall, it is eminently fitted for the town garden, for it is not a straggling plant and rarely requires staking. At Hampton Court Palace it is one of the most striking things in the herbaceous border during July.

The hardy campanulas are good things to have, and in their own shade of blue are not to be beaten; of the taller varieties, the blue and white peach-leaved kinds are the handsomest, and come in very usefully for cutting. *C. carpatica* and *C. c. alba* are shorter, being only one foot high; they flower continuously, and look very well in a bed with the double potentillas, which are described further on.

Coreopsis grandiflora is handsomer than the old *lanceolata*, and bears large bright yellow flowers, which are very handsome when cut and bloom for a long period.

It is difficult to imagine what we should do without delphiniums (larkspurs) in the hardy flower border; they are absolutely invaluable, and seem to have almost every good quality, neither are they at all difficult to grow; some of their blossoms are of an azure blue, a rare colour in nature; then they can be had of a Cambridge blue, purple, white, rose, and even red; the last, however, is a fickle grower and not to be recommended, save for the rockery. Though one may give 21 shillings and even more per dozen for them, beautiful kinds can be had for 10 shillings; these plants run from two to five feet high in good soil, but need plenty of manure to do them really well, as they belong to the tribe of 'gross feeders'.

The erigerons are useful plants to grow, very much like the large-flowered Michaelmas daisies, except that they come in earlier and are of a dwarfer habit; they may be had in orange as well as blue shades.

The funkias are grand plants, grown chiefly for their foliage, which is sometimes green margined with white, or green mixed with gold, and in one kind the leaves are marbled blue and green; they set off the flowers near them to great advantage. In the early spring slugs attack them; these must be trapped and killed (see Chapter 8).

Why are the old Christmas roses seen so little, I wonder? Grown in heavy soil and cold aspect they do beautifully, and bring us their pure white flowers when little else is obtainable outside. One thing against them in this hurry-skurry age is the fact that they increase so slowly; this makes them rather expensive too. Good plants of *helleborus niger maximus* may, however, be bought for half-a-crown; this variety has very handsome leaves, and is all the better for a little manure.

A flower that everybody admires is the *Heuchera sanguinea*, a rare and lovely species; it has graceful sprays of coral-red flowers, borne on stems from one to two feet high, which generally appear in June, and are first rate for cutting. *Lobelia fulgens* is a brilliantly beautiful species, not to be confounded with the dwarf blue kinds; these tall varieties have quaintly-shaped red flowers, and narrow leaves of the darkest crimson; the roots are rather tender, and much dislike damp during the autumn and winter.

Lychnis chalcedonica is one of the unreasonably neglected plants; it has bright scarlet flowers, a good habit, and grows from two to three feet high; it must have a sunny position and prefers a sandy soil.

Some of the new hardy penstemons are lovely, and flower during the whole summer; they look very well in a round bed by themselves, and do not require much looking after; they are rather too tender to withstand our damp winters without protection, therefore the old plants should be mulched, after having had cuttings taken from them, to be kept secure from frost in a frame.

The winter cherry, or Cape gooseberry (*Physalis alkekengi*) is a most fascinating plant; its fruit is the attraction, and resembles Chinese lanterns; they appear early in September, and make quite a good show in the garden. When bad weather comes, the stalks should be cut, hung up to dry for about a week, and then mixed in vases with dried grasses and the effect is very pretty. Care must be taken when asking for this plant under the English name, as there is a greenhouse plant so termed which is quite different, and, of course, will not stand frost. A dozen plants cost about 5 shillings; do not be persuaded to get the newer sort – *franchetti* – the berries are larger, but coarse and flabby, and not nearly so decorative.

Polemonium richardsoni is a very pretty plant, its English name being Jacob's ladder. The flowers are borne in clusters, and are pale sky-blue in colour with a yellow eye: the foliage is fernlike in character and very abundant. This plant likes a shady nook, which must not be under trees, however, and if well watered after its first bloom is over in June, it will flower again in autumn. The double potentillas are glorious things for bedding, and are most uncommon looking. Their flowers are like small double roses in shape: generally orange, scarlet, or a mixture of both: the leaves, greyish-green in colour, resemble those of the strawberry. Unfortunately, these plants require a good deal of staking, but they are well worth the trouble.

The large-leaved saxifrages, sometimes called megaseas, merit a good deal more attention than they receive. For one thing they begin flowering very early, holding up their close pink umbels of flowers so bravely in cold winds: then their foliage is quite distinct, and turns to such a rich red in September that this fact, added to their easy cultivation, makes it wonderful that they are not more grown. I remember, on a dreary day in mid-February, being perfectly charmed by the sight of a large bed of this *saxifraga ligulata*, completely filling up the front garden of a workman's cottage in one of the poorest roads of a large town. The flowers are particularly clean and fresh-looking, and having shiny leaves they of course resist dust and dirt well.

Tradescantias and trollius are two good families of plants for growing on north borders; the first have curious blue or reddish-purple flowers, rising on stiff stalks clothed with long pointed leaves, and they continue in flower from May till September. The trollius has bright orange or lemon-yellow cup-shaped blossoms and luxuriant foliage. It flowers from the end of May for some weeks. Both these plants grow about two feet high.

Violas or tufted pansies are very pretty, and extremely suitable for the ground work of beds, especially where these are in shade, though they will not do under trees. Cuttings must constantly be taken, as one year old plants flower more continuously, and have larger blooms and a more compact habit than older plants, besides which they are apt to die out altogether, if left to themselves.

These are but a few of the wealth of good things to be made use of, for, when once real enthusiasm is awakened, the amateur who wishes to have a thoroughly interesting garden will only be too eager to avail himself of all that is best in the horticultural world.

CHAPTER 5

The Conservatory and Greenhouse

Mistakes in staging ~ Some suitable climbers ~ Economical heating ~ Aspect, shading, etc. ~ The storing of plants ~ No waste space ~ Frames.

A well-kept conservatory adds much to the charm of a drawing room, but requires careful management. Potting and the like cannot very well go on in a place which must always look presentable. A conservatory, of course, is tiled, and therefore every dead leaf and any soil that may be spilled show very much; it is therefore advisable to have a greenhouse as well, or, failing that, some frames. A greenhouse, though it may be only just large enough to turn round in, is a great help towards a nice garden, and a boon in winter; it also allows of a change of plants for the dwelling house and conservatory, greatly to their advantage. Staging generally takes up far too much room; the middle part of a conservatory should be left free, so that there is space to walk about; stands for plants are easily arranged, and give a more natural appearance than fixed staging, which always looks rather stiff. Being a good deal more liable to visits from guests than an ordinary greenhouse, the conservatory must be kept scrupulously clean and neat; the floor, walls, and woodwork must be washed very often, and the glass kept beautifully bright. Cobwebs must never be allowed to settle anywhere, and all the shelves must be kept free of dirt and well painted; curtains should be hung near the entrance to the drawing room, so that they may be pulled across the opening at any time, to hide work of this sort.

Hanging plants are great adjuncts where the structure is lofty, and open-work iron pillars, when draped with some graceful climbing plant, are a great improvement. Where there is but little fire heat, considerable care will be needed to choose something which will look well all the year round. We will suppose that the frost is merely kept out; in the summer, such a house can be bright with plumbago, pelargoniums, salvias, and indeed all the regular greenhouse flowering plants, as, except in hothouses, no artificial heat is then necessary anywhere. In winter, there is more difficulty, for all the climbing plants which are in conspicuous positions must be nearly hardy; of these, the trumpet flower (*Bignonia*), Swainsonia, passionflower, *Choisya ternata*, myrtle and camellia, are the best; these are nearly evergreen, and consequently look ornamental even when out of flower.

Plants suitable for hanging baskets are the trailing tradescantias, the white campanula, lobelia, pelargonium, and many ferns. For the pot plants there are hosts of things; freesias, cyclamen, marguerite-carnations, primulas, Christmas roses, arums, azaleas, kalmias, spireas, chrysanthemums, narcissus, roman hyacinths, and so on. Many late-flowering hardy plants, will, if potted up, continue in bloom long after the cold has cut them off outside.

Cactus plants, too, ordinarily grown in a warm greenhouse, will even withstand one or two degrees of frost when kept perfectly dry, dust-dry, in fact. During winter in England it is the damp that kills, not the cold; bearing that in mind, we shall be able to grow many things that hitherto have puzzled us. All those delicate iris, half-hardy ferns, and tiresome plants that would put off flowering till too late, why, a cold conservatory or greenhouse is the very place for them!

Greenhouses are altogether easier to manage than conservatories, and therefore are the best for amateurs. There cuttings may be struck, plants repotted, fuchsias, geraniums, etc., stored, and tender annuals reared. A lean-to greenhouse should face south preferably, and the door should be placed at the warm end, that is, the west, so that when opened no biting wind rushes in. When the summer comes, a temporary shading will be necessary; twopennyworth of whitening and a little water mixed into a paste will do this. About the middle of September it should be washed off, if the rain has not already done so; for if it remains on too long the plants will grow pale and lanky.

Artificial heat

The Rippingille stove before referred to must be placed at the coldest end, and only sufficient warmth should emanate from it just to keep out the frost, unless it is intended to use it all day. It is well to remember that the colder the atmosphere outside, the cooler in proportion must the interior be. Even a hothouse is allowed by a good gardener to go down to 60° or even 55° on a bitterly cold night, as a great amount of fire heat at such times is inimical to plant life, though it will stand a tremendous amount of sunpower. Several mats or lengths of woollen material, canvas, etc., stretched along outside will save expense, and be a more natural way of preserving the plants.

One great advantage that a greenhouse has over a conservatory is this: that any climbers can be planted out, whereas tubs have to be used where the floor is tiled. Cucumbers and tomatoes do very well in a small house, and an abundance of these is sure to please the housekeeper. Seeds of the cucumber should be sown about the first week in March on a hotbed; if in small pots all the better, as their roots suffer less when transferred to where they are to fruit. Do not let the shoots become crowded, or insects and mildew will attack them. In the summer, 'damp down' pretty frequently and give plenty of air, avoiding anything like a draught, however. 'Telegraph', though not new, is a reliable cucumber of good flavour and a first rate cropper. Tomato seed should be sown about the same time and the plants treated similarly, giving plenty of water but no stimulant in the way of guano till they have set their fruit, which can be assisted by passing a camel's hair brush over the flowers, and thus fertilising them. Of course, out of doors the bees do this; their 'busyness' materially aiding the gardener.

As to storing plants, a box of sand placed in a dry corner where no drip can reach it, is best for this, burying the roots of dahlias, etc., fairly deep in it, and withholding water till the spring, when they may be taken out, each root examined, decayed parts removed, and every healthy plant repotted. The pots should be placed under the shelves till they shoot forth, when they can be gradually brought forward to the light. This reminds me that the dark parts of a greenhouse should never be wasted, as, besides their use in bringing up bulbs, ferns can be grown for cutting, and such things as rhubarb, may be readily forced there. Frames are very useful and fairly cheap, though it is best to get them set with 21 oz. glass, or they will not last long. Seedlings may be brought up in them with greater success than if in a greenhouse, and a supply of violets may be kept up in them during the coldest weather. The mats they are covered with during the night must never be removed till the frost is well off the grass, say about 11 a.m., as a sudden thaw makes terrible havoc.

The great point to remember when about to indulge in a greenhouse is this: unless sufficient time and trouble can be given to make it worth while, it is better to spend the money on the outdoor department, which to a certain extent takes care of itself. Where there is leisure to attend to a greenhouse, however, few things will give more return for the care spent on it.

CHAPTER 6

The Tool Shed and Summer House

Spades and the Bishop ~ Weeding without backache ~ The indispensable thermometer ~ Well-made tools a necessity ~ Summer houses and their adornment.

Though it is true enough that the best workmen need little mechanical aid, yet a well-stocked tool shed is not to be despised. Sometimes it may only be a portion of a bicycle shed which can be set apart for our implements, or the greenhouse may have to find room for a good many of them, but certain it is that a few nicely finished tools are an absolute necessity to the would-be gardener. Of course a good many of them can be hired; it is not everyone, for instance, who possesses a lawn mower, but if the owner of a garden is ambitious enough to wish to do without a gardener altogether, a lawn mower will be one of the first things he will wish to possess himself of. In that case he cannot do better than invest is one of Ransome's or Green's machines. Their work is always of a high standard and the firms are constantly making improvements in them. The newest ones are almost perfection, but it is better to get a second-hand one of either of these firms than a new one of an inferior make. A roller is useful too, but, as these large implements run into a good deal of money, it may be as well to state that, on payment of 2 pence or so, any of them may be borrowed for an hour or two. Ladders can be had in this way; also shears, fret-saws – anything that is only wanted occasionally.

A spade is a daily necessity, however. Has not one of our most learned divines exalted the art of digging by his commendation thereof, and who shall say him nay? It is expedient to wear thick boots, however, during this operation, not only on account of the earth's moisture, but also because otherwise it is ruinous to our soles. To preserve the latter, a spade with a sharp edge should never be chosen, but one which has a flat piece of iron welded on to the body of it. Digging is good because it breaks up the earth, and exposes it to the sun and also to the frost, which sweetens and purifies it; care must be taken however, in doing it, as so many things die down in the winter and are not easily seen. The ordinary hired gardener is very clever at burying things so deep that they never come up again!

Most people abhor weeding, yet if done with a Dutch hoe it is rather pleasant work, as no stooping is required. After a few showers of rain the hoe runs along very easily, and the good it does is so patent that I always think it very satisfactory labour indeed. These hoes cost about 1 shilling 6 pence each.

Raking is easy work, and very useful for smoothing beds or covering seeds over with soil. English made, with about eight or ten teeth, their cost is from two to three shillings. One of the most necessary implements is a trowel, in particular for a lady, as its use does not need so much muscle as a spade; their price is from 1 shilling 6 pence to 2 shillings 6 pence each.

Where there are many climbers a hammer is wanted, not a toy one of German make; these are sometimes chosen by amateurs under the mistaken idea that the lighter the hammer the lighter the work. One of English make, strong and durable, is the kind of thing required, and costs about 2 shillings or 2 shillings 6 pence. Wall nails, one inch long (the most useful size), are 2 pence a pound, and may be had at any ironmongers. The shreds of cloth may be bought too, but anyone who deals at a tailor's can procure a mixed bundle of cloth pieces for nothing, when there is the light labour of cutting them into shreds, work of a few minutes only.

In choosing watering cans, see that they are thoroughly good tin, as a strong can will last for years; moreover, when it begins to leak it will bear mending; they cost from 3 shillings upwards, the roses should be made to take off as a rule, and a special place assigned to them on the shelf of the toolshed, as they readily get lost. Syringes, much used for washing off insects, are rather expensive, consequently are not to be found in many small gardens; a more fortunate friend will sometimes lend one, as there is a good deal of freemasonry amongst people who indulge in the hobby of gardening.

A thing everyone must have is a thermometer, in greenhouses they are indispensable; the minimum kind are the most useful, telling one as they do exactly the degree of frost experienced during the preceding night. They may be bought at a chemist's for 1s. each, and must be reset every day; the aforesaid chemist will show any purchaser the way to do this – it is quite simple.

Raffia, or bass, for tying flower sticks, and labels are minor necessities which cost little, though sticks may run into a good deal if bought prepared for staking. Personally, I dislike both the coloured kinds (never Nature's green) and the white. Both show far more than the unobtrusive sticks obtained by cutting down the stalks of Michaelmas daisies, for instance. Galvanised iron stakes last practically for ever, and if they are of the twisted kind, no tying is required, greatly lessening labour. It is a curious fact that though arches made of iron set up electrical disturbance and injure the climbers, these stakes seem to have no bad effect whatever. At the end of the autumn they should be collected, and stored in a safe place till summer comes round again. Thin ones suitable for carnations, etc., may be procured from A. Porter, Storehouse, Maidstone, for 1 shilling a dozen, carriage paid. The thicker ones can be made to order at small cost at any ironmonger's.

A handy man can often make frames himself, especially if they are not required to be portable, and really these homemade ones answer almost as well as those that are bought. Good frames can sometimes be had at sales for an old song, and only require a coat of paint to make them as good as new.

Here I will end my list, only reiterating that, however few tools you may have, it is foolish to get any but the best.

A summer house need not necessarily be bought ready-made. I have seen many a pretty bower put together in the spare hours of the carpenter of the family. There is one advantage in these homemade summer houses, that they are generally more roomy than those which are bought, and can be made to suit individual requirements.

How to cover a summer house

Of course, it is more necessary to cover these amateur and therefore somewhat clumsy structures with creepers, but that is not difficult. Even the first summer they can be made to look quite presentable by planting the Japanese hop. The leaves are variegated, and in shape like the Virginia creeper. Messrs. Barr, of Long Ditton, Surrey, told me it grew 25 feet in one season. It can be had from them in pots, about the first week in May, for 3 shillings 6 pence a dozen. Then there are the nasturtiums, always so effective when trained up lengths of string, with the dark background of the summer house to show up their beautiful flowers. If the soil in which they grow is poor and gravelly, the blossoms will be more numerous. The canary creeper is another plant, which is so airy and graceful that one never seems to tire of it. Get the seeds up in good time, so that when planted out they are of a fair height, else so much of the summer is lost.

There are so many uncommon climbing plants which should be tried, notably *eccremocarpus scaber*, *cobea scandens*, and *mina lobata*. The last two are annual, and the first can be grown as such, though in mild winters and in sunny positions it is a perennial. It flowers whenever the weather will let it, and its blossoms are orange-yellow in colour, very curious and invariably noticed by visitors. Reliable seeds of all three can be had from Messrs. Barr, at 6 pence a packet. The *cobea* bears pale purple bell-shaped flowers, and is a quick grower. *Mina lobata* is generally admired, and though of a different family bears a slight resemblance to an *eccremocarpus*, both in the shape of its flowers and in the way they are arranged on the stem. It is only half hardy. *Clematis jackmanni* and *montana* are good for this position too. *Jackmanni* is the well-known velvety purple kind, and must be cut down to the ground every autumn, and well mulched; that is because it flowers on the new growth of each year. Montana, however, flowers on the wood of the previous year, and therefore must be cut back about the end of June, if at all, as May is the month it blooms.

The Dutchman's pipe, or *Aristolochia sipho*, is not to be altogether recommended, as its huge leaves always seem to make small gardens appear smaller still, which is not desirable; otherwise, it is a splendid plant for covering summer houses, as it is a rapid climber. It is wise to plant some of the decorative ivies as well, so that, if the flowering plants fail, it will not be of so much consequence. The varieties with pointed leaves are exceedingly elegant, and are much more suitable than the common sort for decorating churches and dwelling house, and cost no more to buy.

Fragrant odours

At the base of the summer house there should be quantities of sweet-scented plants, as this will make the time spent there all the pleasanter. There are lavender, rosemary, thyme, bay, sweet peas, stocks, and mignonette, besides the oak-leaved geranium, tobacco plant, marvel of Peru, and, of course, roses, though the latter do not give off scent quite so much as the other plants mentioned.

The position of the summer house is important. I have seen some divided, but where there is no partition it should generally face west. It is delightful on a fine evening to sit and watch the clouds change from glory to glory, as the sun gradually sinks to its rest, and the stars gleam out in the darkening sky.

CHAPTER 7

Roses for Amateurs

Teas ~ Hybrid perpetuals ~ Some good climbing varieties ~ Treatment and soil ~ Rose hedges ~ Pillar roses.

The reason for the heading given to this chapter is that growing roses for show will not be mentioned, as it is quite a separate branch of the art and would require a book to itself to do it full justice. Blooms of a fair size, but in abundance during five months of the year, that is what most amateurs need, for, after all, the amount of disbudding that has to be done when growing roses for show quite goes to one's heart! We want fine, well-coloured, healthy flowers, and to attain that end a good soil is absolutely necessary. This is especially the case with Hybrid Perpetuals, but Teas will often do in a light soil, if manure is given them, and plenty of water in the dry season. The H.P.'s, as gardeners call them, must have loam and clay to do them properly; where the soil is not improved by adding these ingredients, it is advisable to rely chiefly on Tea roses.

The advantages of teas

For many reasons Tea roses are the best for small gardens, as they like the shelter found there. They flower more continuously and in much greater profusion, are not so troubled with green fly, and are far more decorative in habit of growth and colour of leafage than most of the other species. In their particular shades of colour they cannot be equalled, though for cherry reds and dark maroons we have to look to the Hybrid Perpetual, at least, if we want flowers of fine form, and also for that lovely fresh pink of the Captain Christy type (though this is now termed a Hybrid Tea by rosarians). The name Perpetual is apt to give a false idea to those who are not experienced. Most of these roses are not at all continuous, many only lasting six weeks or so in bloom, and some even less, if the season is hot; that is one great reason why they are being superseded by Teas, at least in the suburbs of London and the South of England. In the Midlands and North the hardiness of the H.P.'s is greatly in their favour.

Teas will stand the closeness of a garden surrounded by houses and trees much better than the Perpetuals, which are very apt to become mildewed in such positions. Of course, many remedies are given for this, but often they are worse than the disease;

flowers of sulphur, for instance, to take the best-known remedy, disfigures the whole plant terribly.

Teas are much the best for planting in beds which are very conspicuous, for, as I said previously, they are always ornamental. Where standards are placed down each side of the lawn, it is rather a good plan to place all the Hybrid Perpetuals on one side and the Teas on the other, giving the greater amount of sun to the latter.

Good climbers for warm walls

When covering a very hot wall, too, it is best, in the South of England, to stick to the tender roses, as the others become almost burnt up. I will name here five of the best climbing Tea roses for a south or west wall. William Allan Richardson the beautiful orange variety so much admired; Bouquêt d'or, a daughter of Gloire de Dijon, but prettier in the bud than the old variety; Madame Berard, fawny yellow, very floriferous; L'Idéal, and Gustave Regis. L'Idéal is a most beautiful rose, its colouring almost defying description – a peculiar yellow, streaked with red and gold, like a Turner sunset. Gustave Regis, though often classed as a bush rose, easily covers a low wall, and is one of the best kinds there are, as it is covered with bloom the whole of the season. The buds make lovely buttonholes, and are creamy yellow, long, and pointed. They are just like waterlilies when fully open, and on a warm sunny day exhale a perfectly delicious fragrance, unlike any other rose with which I am acquainted.

Another good climbing tea rose is Duchesse d'Auerstadt. Though introduced as long ago as 1887, this variety is not often heard of, perhaps on account of its shy blooming qualities. This however need deter no one from growing it, as its lovely foliage makes it quite a picture at all times: bronze, crimson, rich metallic green, its shoots and leaves are a pleasure to look at. Its flowers, too, when they come, how splendid they are! great golden goblets full to overflowing with the firm, rich petals and with a scent to match; they are indeed worth waiting for! Anxiously is each bud watched, for they take so long to come to perfection that the anxiety is not ill-founded. I have known a bud take four weeks to come out, but then it had to stand a lot of bad weather, and came through it safely after all. All these rose trees may be had from Benjamin R. Cant & Sons, Colchester, at 1 shilling 6 pence each. This firm always sends out good plants, with plenty of vitality in them, and as these old-established rose nurseries are by no means in a sheltered spot, you may be sure of each tree being hardily grown and thoroughly ripened, great points in their future well-being.

Climbers for cool walls

East, or better still E.S.E., is a good aspect for Hybrid Perpetual and Bourbon roses on walls. I have frequently noticed that they have a great dislike to the very hottest of the sun's rays, and that is the reason I have advised those places to be reserved for Teas. Some good climbing varieties for cool aspects are: Mrs. John Laing, a satiny pink of lovely form and sweet scent. Jules Margottin, cherry-red, globular in shape, sweet-scented and very floriferous. Prince Camille de Rohan, one of the best dark roses to be had, as they are generally so difficult to grow – it is blackish-maroon in colour, and flowers abundantly. Boule-de-neige, a Bourbon, with white flowers in great abundance. Madame Isaac Pereire another Bourbon; it is a quick grower and most abundant flowerer, the flowers are bright rose crimson. Souvenir-de-la-Malmaison, one of the best Bourbons we have; does particularly well on cold walls, even on those facing north. Its flowers are very large, somewhat flat in form, and blush-white; it blooms abundantly in autumn, and is rarely subject to blight.

Climbers require very little pruning

It is a case chiefly of cutting out all dead wood, and

snipping the decayed ends of those that are left. When planting rose trees of any description, choose mild and if possible calm weather, for it is better to keep the trees out of the ground a few days rather than plant them in frosty weather. The soil should be friable, so that it crumbles fairly well, and when the plant is in position it is advisable to cover the roots with potting soil for two or three inches. Spread the roots out like a fan, and be sure not to plant the tree too deep. Look carefully for the mark showing the union of graft and stock, and be careful not to cover this with more than two inches of soil. Tread down the soil well to make it firm, and thus induce the rose trees to make fresh roots. In planting out climbers, carefully tack all loose shoots to the wall or fence behind it, else the wind may do much harm. When all is finished give a good mulching of strawy manure, which should be dug in when March comes; and if there is a likelihood of frost, protect the branches with bracken or any light covering.

Bush roses of the H.P. type

I will now give a few of the best Hybrid Perpetuals of the bush type; many of the varieties I shall name, however, make very good standards though they are more expensive. The 'dwarfs', as rosarians call them, only cost from 9 pence to 1 shilling each at Messrs. Cant's, except in the case of novelties; and where these are concerned, it is well to wait a year or two, as they rapidly go down to the normal price. Duke of Teck, bright carmine scarlet, of good form, and occasionally blooms in the autumn. Dupuy Jamain, one of the best H.P.'s ever introduced, the flowers are almost cherry-red in colour, sweet-scented, and come out in succession the whole of the summer: it is a quick grower, and does well in a somewhat shady position. Heinrich Schultheis flowers of a true rose-pink touched with silver, very prettily shaped and exceedingly fragrant. Unfortunately, this variety is subject to attacks of mildew, though this does not seem to affect the beauty of the flowers but spoils the leaves.

Baroness Rothschild, a faultless rose as regards form and colour, which is a beautiful pale pink, but utterly devoid of scent, a serious fault in my opinion. Comtesse de Bearn, large, dark, and very floriferous. Madame Gabriel Luizet, light silvery pink, quick growing, and free blooming. Ulrich Brunner, always given an excellent character in the catalogues, and indeed it is a good rose, cherry-red in colour, sweet-scented, and of fine form: it rarely ails, mildew and rust passing it by altogether. It is exceedingly vigorous, and makes therefore a good pillar rose. Pride of Waltham, a rose little heard-of yet most lovely; its blossoms are of the brightest pink, sweetly scented, and beautifully cupped. Charles Lefèvre, beautiful crimson with dark shading; also very good at Kew (and continuous). Abel Carrière, another dark maroon of fine form, and Queen of the bedders, producing carmine flowers so freely that it must be disbudded; it is subject to mildew.

So many roses formerly classed as Hybrid Perpetuals are now called Hybrid Teas. The dear old La France is one that has undergone this change; it is a rose no one should be without, and should be grown both as a standard and a bush; its silvery pink flowers have a most exquisite scent and perfect shape (that is, when nearly wide open; it is not a good buttonhole variety). Another Hybrid Tea rose that has come to the fore lately is Bardou Job, a splendid bedding variety, with flaming roses almost single in form, but produced in prodigal profusion; it pays for feeding. Queen Mab is a somewhat similar rose but has apricot flowers, tinted pink and orange, borne in the same generous manner. It is a china rose; neither of these kinds attain a great height, nevertheless beds entirely composed of them are exceedingly effective and may be seen some distance off; they require very little pruning.

Pillar roses

Having mentioned pillar roses, I will add a few more names especially calculated to do well in such positions; perhaps one of the best is Paul's Carmine Pillar, with its sheets; of lovely flowers covering the stems the whole way up, with plenty of healthy foliage to set them off. When better known, I should imagine it would be a rival even to Turner's Crimson Rambler, magnificent as that is when grown to perfection. At Kew recently a bed of the Carmine Pillar was quite one of the sights of the garden. A close investigation of the bed in which they were planted revealed the fact that every alternate rose tree was a Gloire de Dijon, but each one was a sorry failure, and instead of scaling the heights, crouched low at the foot of its iron stake, as though unwilling to compete with the other blushing occupants. The 'glories' were not very youthful either, that one could see by their thick hard stems; plenty of time had evidently been given them to do the work, but for some unknown reason they had shirked it. I have known several cases of this sort with the much-loved 'glory de John', as the gardeners broadly term it. Madame Plantier is a good white pillar rose, doing well in any situation, and Cheshunt Hybrid is also most accommodating, and blooms well even in poor soil, though it well repays good cultivation. Its flowers, cherry-carmine in colour, are large and full, and the petals are prettily veined and curl over at the edges. The foliage is rich, and the tree never seems attacked by any disease; it is a Hybrid Tea. Aimée Vibert, a noisette, is very good as a pillar rose and extremely hardy; it also does well on arches; the flowers are small and white, with pink tips to the petals; it is very free, and flowers continuously.

Rose hedges

Hedges of roses are quite as effective as pillars, and make a very pretty screen for two thirds of the year. The evergreen roses are best for this purpose, and of these Flora is by far-and-away the nicest rose. It has sweet flowers, small, full, and of the loveliest pink; they are borne in clusters, each one looking just ready for a fairy-wedding bouquet. They have a delightful scent, too, their only fault being their short duration; in one summer they will grow from five to ten feet, and are so free-flowering as almost to hide the leaves. Dundee Rambler, Ruga, Mirianthes, and Léopoldine d'Orléans are all equally suitable for hedges.

Dwarf teas

I will now name a list of the best dwarf Tea roses; to begin with, Alba Rosea is a dear old rose tree, moderate in growth, bearing numbers of flesh-white blossoms, good in form though small in size. These have a faint, sweet scent, and are very pretty for cutting. One day last August, I cut a whole branch off with about six open flowers upon it, and put it in a tall vase just as it was; they arranged themselves, and were much admired. The tree is decidedly dwarf and moderate in growth, and the leaves are very dark green, thus making a beautiful foil to the roses. Catherine Mermet is somewhat of the same type, but the flowers are larger and more deeply flushed with pink; it is a good greenhouse rose. Madame de Watteville resembles a tulip, having thick firm petals of a creamy-white colour, distinctly edged with pink. It is a strong grower and free in flowering. Madame Hoste is a pretty lemon-yellow colour, one of the easiest to grow in this particular shade; the flowers are of good form, and if well manured are large and full; it has a sweet scent. Madame Lambard is a rose no one can do without, it is so free-blooming and continuous; the colour is not constant, sometimes being mostly pink, at others almost a fawn, but as a rule it is a blend of those two shades.

Marie van Houtte is another indispensable variety; the roses are lovely in form, of a pale lemon-yellow colour, each petal being flushed with pink at the edges, and the whole having a soft bloom, as it were, over it. This carmine marking, however, is not constant; weather and position seem to have a good deal to do with it. Meteor is one of the darker Teas, being carmine-crimson shaded with blackish-maroon; the roses are not full though of good shape, consequently they look best in bud. This tree wants feeding to do well, and is not a vigorous grower. Grace Darling is a gem which everyone should have; the blossoms are large, full, perfect in shape and exquisite in colour, which is generally a peachy-pink, the reverse of the petals being a rich cream, and, as these curl over in a charming manner, the effect is unique and extremely beautiful. The foliage is abundant, of a ruddy tint, and keeps free from blight; indeed, this entirely fascinating rose has only one fault, it is altogether too unassuming.

A bright, pink rose of fine form is the Duchess of Albany; it is often called a deep coloured La France, as it is a 'sport' from that famous rose. The Marquis of Salisbury is another dark tea rose; it is small but well-shaped though thin, and the blooms are abundant; it is strictly moderate in growth, being somewhat like the Chinas in habit. A fine rose in a warm summer is Kaiserin Friedrich, as it has large, very full, flowers, which take a good deal of building up; it appears to dislike cold and rainy weather.

Sunrise is a new kind that is making a considerable stir in the rose world; its flowers vary from reddish-carmine to pale fawn, and the tree has glorious foliage.

The time to plant

October and November are the best months to plant rose trees, except in very cold parts; February is then a safer time, especially for the tender sorts. Their first season they require a great deal of looking after; their roots have not got a proper foothold in the earth, and this means constant watering in dry weather. At blooming time, an occasional application of guano does a great deal of good, making both flowers and leaves richer in colour. Dead blooms, too, must be sedulously cut off, as, if left on, the tree is weakened.

Pruning

Do a little pruning in October, though March and April are the chief months. In the autumn, however, the shoots of rose trees should be thinned out, the branches left can then be shortened a fourth of their length with advantage, as the winter's howling winds are less likely to harm them. Standards especially require this, as when 'carrying much sail' they are very liable to be uprooted.

When the spring comes, look the trees carefully over before commencing operations, remembering that the sturdier a tree is the less it needs pruning. The knife must go the deepest in the case of the poor, weak ones. Always prune down to an 'eye', that is an incipient leaf bud; if this is not done the wood rots.

Evergreen roses need scarcely be touched, save to cut out dead branches and snip off decayed ends.

For Teas and Noisettes also, little actual pruning is necessary. H.P.'s require the most. As a general rule for roses, if you want quality, not quantity, prune hard, but to enable you to 'cut and come again', only prune moderately.

Dis-budding is a certain method of improving the blooms if it is done in time. It is little use to do it when the buds once begin to show colour; start picking off the superfluous ones when they are quite small, and the difference in size and shape is often amazing.

CHAPTER 8

Enemies of the Garden

Slugs, and how to trap them ~ Blight or green fly ~ Earwigs ~ Wireworm ~ Snails ~ Mice ~ Friends mistakenly called foes.

The best garden as a rule has the fewest insects, indeed, no foe is allowed to lodge for any length of time without means being taken for its extermination. Some enemies are more easily got rid of than others; for instance, green fly, or aphis (to give it the scientific name), rarely attacks healthy plants to any extent; it goes for the sick ones, therefore good cultivation will speedily reduce their numbers. When any is seen, a strong syringing of soapy water will generally dislodge them, or, if this is impracticable, a dusting of tobacco powder is a very good substitute. Tait and Buchanan's Anti-blight, to be had of most seedsmen, is a reliable powder; it is also efficacious in preventing mildew in potatoes, chrysanthemums, etc.

In some gardens, especially those inclined to be damp, slugs are very troublesome; their depredations are usually carried on by night, so that it is rather difficult to trap them; many things are sold for this purpose, but hand-picking is the surest method. In the evening, sink a saucer a little way in the border, and fill this with moist bran; it is irresistible to the slugs, and when twilight comes on they will steal out from their hiding places and make a supper off it. Then comes man's opportunity. Armed with a pointed stick and a pail of salt and water, they must be picked off and popped into the receptacle, there to meet a painless death; one can squash them under foot, but where they are plentiful this is rather a messy proceeding. Snails may be trapped in exactly the same way; salt or sand should be placed in a ring round any plant they are specially fond of, or else in a single night they will graze off the whole of the juicy tops. Young growths are their greatest delicacy, hence they are most troublesome in the spring.

Wireworm is another tiresome enemy well known to carnation growers, and more difficult to get rid of than the slug, owing to its hard and horny covering which resists crushing; salt again, however, is a splendid cure. It should be well mixed with the soil though not brought too close to the plants. Earwigs are horrid insects to get into a garden; they often come in with a load of manure, simply swarms of them imbedding themselves in such places. Dahlias are the plants they like best, and, if not kept down with a watchful eye, they will completely spoil both flowers and leaves. Hollow tubes, such as short straws, put round will collect many, or the old plan of filling an inverted flowerpot with moss is also useful, though somewhat disfiguring, if perched on the tops of the stakes supporting the dahlias.

Mice are dreadfully destructive, too, especially in the country, and being so quick in their movements they are troublesome to catch. Traps must be baited with the daintiest morsels, to make them turn away from the succulent tops of the new vegetation. Owls and other large birds are most effectual in doing away with these troublesome little animals, a fact which should be taken into account. Many people from ignorance destroy birds or insects which may be urgently required to keep down annoying pests – take, for instance, ladybirds – the pretty creatures are invaluable where there is much green fly, yet how often are they doomed to death by some well-meaning gardener, and it is the same with birds. A robin or sparrow will eat hundreds of aphides in one day, so that, unless there are many fruit trees in the garden, it is most unwise to shoot the dear little songsters; and even in the latter case, if protection can be afforded, by all means save the birds! A while ago some farmers had been so enraged by the devastation made by the sparrows and starlings that they determined to kill all the old birds. The consequence was that they were so overrun the next season by insects of every description, that they had to import birds at great trouble, to take the place of those they had killed. Foes are often mistaken for friends, but occasionally the reverse is the case!

CHAPTER 9

The Rockery

A few hints on its construction ~ Aspect and soil ~ A list of Alpines ~ Other suitable plants.

A well-constructed rockery filled with a good selection of Alpine plants is a never-failing delight to anyone fond of a garden. Yet how rare a thing it is! Most of the erections one sees are mere apologies for the real thing. The truth is not one gardener in a hundred knows how to make a rockery, though he does not like to say so! An artistic mind is needed to construct one that will be pleasing to the eye, besides a knowledge of draining, water supply, and so forth. An educated person is not actually necessary, but one with common sense, who would not dream of making it merely another background for gorgeous bedding plants which are all very well in their right place, but absolutely unsuited to a rockery.

As regards aspect, one that is built on each side of a narrow path running north and south, does very well, but as this may be impossible in a small garden, a corner rockery built high in the form of a triangle and facing south-east, can be made extremely pretty, as I know from experience. Where the rockery is in the shade, no overhanging trees must be near, if choice Alpines are expected to live there.

The material may be either slabs of grey stone as at Kew, or the more easily obtained 'clinkers'. Clinkers are really bricks spoiled in the baking, having all sorts of excrescences on them which unfit them for ordinary building purposes; they should always be ordered from a strictly local contractor, as carriage adds considerably to the cost.

The soil should be a mixture of peat, sand, and loam; no manure should be incorporated, the 'pockets' for special favourites and plants that have individual wants can be filled in at the time of planting. One advantage pertaining to a rockery is that many plants which quite refuse to thrive in a border will grow and flourish there, and the attention they need is less troublesome to give; in fact, it is a delightful form of gardening, especially for a lady, as there is no fear of the feet getting dirty or wet, and a trowel, not a spade, is the chief implement used. A small piece of turf, just a few feet wide, at the bottom of the corner style of rockery, is a great set-off, and a vast improvement on a gravel path.

Suitable plants for a rockery

The following are some of the best flowers for a rockery. The aubrietias are very pretty little plants, having creeping rosettes of greyish-green leaves, and a perfect sheet of mauve or lilac bloom about April. The effect is greatly enhanced when planted so as to fall over a stone or brick; indeed, it is for those things which are so easily lost sight of in a border that a rockery comes in; they can be closely inspected there without much stooping.

The arabis is a pretty plant, somewhat like the aubrietia in habit and time of flowering; hence, where only a small selection can be made, it might be left out, as it is a trifle coarse. Such a term could never be applied to the androsaces, which may be numbered among the elite of rock plants; they are evergreens, and do not exceed six inches in height; they bear tiny but very bright flowers, varying from rose in some species to lavender in others.

Appenine gems

Some of the alpine anemones are lovely, notably *A. appennina*, which has sky-blue flowers that open out flat on very short stalks, surrounded by pale green denticulated foliage. *A. blanda* is much the same, save that it flowers a month or so earlier; they are spring-blooming plants, and like moisture and shade, and will not do at all if subjected to much hot sun. These and many similar plants can often be planted on a rockery facing south-east (which aspect suits so many sunloving plants), by arranging bricks, stones, or small shrubs, so as to shelter them from its hottest rays. Aquilegias, mentioned in the list of border plants, look quite as well on a rockery, if moisture can be given them, as their flowers are so delicate, and the leaves so fragile and prettily coloured, especially in the early spring. The blue and white *A. cærulea*, from the Rocky Mountains, is a gem, and the scarlet kinds are very effective.

For forming close green carpets, *Arenaria balearica* is most useful; it creeps over rocks and stones, covering them completely with its moss-like growth, and hiding any hard, unlovely surfaces. The campanula family is a host in itself, many of the smaller varieties looking better on a rockery than anywhere else. Some of these tiny bell flowers have, however, the very longest of names! *C. portenschlagiana*, for instance, is only four inches high, and a charming little plant it is, and flowers for months, beginning about July. The blossoms are purple-blue in colour, and continue right into November, unless very hard frosts come to stop it. *C. cespetosa* is another variety well suited to rockwork, as it is even smaller than the last.

The alpine wallflower, *Cheiranthus alpinus*, is a very choice little plant; it has creamy-yellow flowers, borne on stalks a few inches high, and, though each individual plant is biennial, they seed so freely that they are practically perennial. A light, dry soil and a sunny situation suits them; they will even grow on old walls, and very picturesque they look perched up on some mossy old ruin.

An attractive rock plant, though rarely seen, is *Chrysogonum virginianum*; its flowers are creamy-yellow, and grow in a very quaint manner; this plant blooms the whole season through. Plants of this character should be noted carefully, as they help to give a rockery a well-furnished appearance, so that one always has something to show visitors.

For warm, dry, sunny nooks rock roses are the very thing; where other plants would be burnt up, the cistus flourishes, for it requires no particular depth of soil. *C. florentinus* (white) and *C. crispus* (dark crimson), are two of the best.

One of the most exquisite and interesting rock plants I have ever seen is *Clematis davidiana*, a plant only introduced of recent years, but noticeable wherever seen; it is not a climber, as its name might lead one to suppose, for it only grows two feet high, and generally trails along the ground; the flowers are curious in shape, and of a metallic blue-grey colour; the foliage is very neat and pretty; it blooms about July, and should be planted so that it can be examined closely.

The fumitories are elegant plants, and nearly always in flower; the blossoms are small, yellow, sometimes white, and borne in profusion amongst the finely cut foliage, which, the whole summer through, is a bright clear green. With one plant of *corydalis lutea* a stock can soon be obtained, as this variety seeds freely. All the fumitories prefer a light soil and a sunny position.

Dwarf evergreen shrubs greatly improve the appearance of the rockery in late autumn and winter, especially when they add berries to their attractions. The cotoneasters are evergreen, and when about a foot high are very suitable for such a position. *C. horizontalis* and *C. micicrophylla* bear scarlet berries, and are altogether very choice; they must not be allowed to get too large, but taken up when little over a foot high, and others substituted for them.

Various bulbs, which we generally plant in the border, find a prettier background in the rockery; here each bulb is made the most of, and, where very small, is seen to greater advantage; even if ever so insignificant, it cannot get buried away under a spadeful of soil, nor get splashed with mud. You must often have noticed how crocuses get blown over and spoilt by the wind, but in a cosy nook of the rockwork, planted fairly close together, and in a 'pocket' surrounded by bricks, they find a happy home, and can be inspected without any difficulty. Personally, I do not care for crocuses in a line; one cannot see their pure transparency, and only get an idea of a broad band of colour; close at hand, their dewy chalices, exquisitely veined and streaked, seem far more beautiful, particularly where the finer sorts are selected. All crocuses do not flower in spring; some of the prettiest species bloom in autumn, though many people, seeing them at that time, imagine they are colchicums; the latter, though certainly very decorative when in flower, are followed by such coarse leaves that the crocus is decidedly preferable.

The hardy cyclamen are very suitable for a rockery, as, being beauties in miniature, they are apt to get lost in a mixed border. *C. neapolitanum* has marbled foliage and pretty pink flowers, and *C. europeum* (maroonish crimson) is also well worth growing; they must be placed in a shady part, yet where the drainage is perfect; stagnant moisture kills them.

The hardy orchids should be tried too, especially the cypripedium; it is not generally known how handsome some of them are; they like shade and moisture; indeed, through the summer the peat they are growing in should be a regular swamp, or they will fail to produce fine flowers.

Another plant that likes peat is the little *Daphne eneorum*. This is an evergreen, and produces its pink fragrant flowers every spring; it will not do in very smoky places, but, like the heath, must have a fairly pure atmosphere.

The alpine pinks are treasures for the rockery, and do well in town gardens; they flower nearly all the summer, and are not particular as to soil and position, though they prefer plenty of sun.

The gentians look very well on rockwork, but like a stronger soil than most alpines, loam suiting them best. Water should be generously given during spring and summer. *G. acaulis* is the best for amateurs.

The red shades found in the geum tribe are very uncommon, being neither crimson, scarlet, nor orange, but a mixture of all three, with a dash of brown thrown in. They flower continuously, and have dull green woolly foliage, which sets the flowers off well. They need a light, well-drained soil. *Geum chilense,* or *Coccineum plenum*, is a good kind, and so is *G. miniatum*; both are about two feet high, but require no staking whatever. Of course, it will be understood that sticks, except of the lightest kind, are quite inadmissible on a rockery.

Helianthemums, or rock roses, are charming little evergreen plants, with wiry prostrate stems, and small flowers, which are freely produced all the summer. They may be had in white, yellow, pink, scarlet, and crimson, and either double or single; the variety named Mrs. C. W. Earle is a very effective double scarlet, and quite a novelty.

Iris reticulata is a very fascinating little bulbous plant, well adapted for a rockery; it blooms in the early spring, and very beautiful the flowers are, being rich violet-purple, with gold blotches on each petal; they are scented, too; when in blossom, the stems reach to about nine inches in height.

One of the most lovely plants that can be imagined for a rockery is *lithospermum prostratum*, and yet how rarely one sees it; the glossy green leaves always look cheerful, and the flowers are exquisite, they are a bright full blue, and each petal is slightly veined with red, it is not difficult to grow, a dry, sunny position being all it requires; it is of trailing habit and an evergreen. Everyone knows the creeping jenny, but it is not to be despised for rockwork, especially for filling up odd corners where other things will not thrive. It blooms best where there is a certain amount of sun.

St. Dabeoc's Heath is a pretty little shrub, very neat and of good habit; its flowers are the true pink, shading off to white, and of the well-known heath shape. Somewhat slow-growing, it prefers peat.

Plants that flower the whole season through are most valuable on the rockery. Œnotheras may be depended on to present a pleasing appearance for several weeks, especially if all dead flowers are picked off. The dwarf kinds are the most suitable, such as *Oenothera marginata*, *missouriensis*, *linearis*, and *taraxacifolia*. The last named, however, is only a biennial, but has the advantage of opening in the morning, while most of the evening primroses do not seem to think it worth while to make themselves attractive till calling hours.

The most fairy-like little plant for filling up narrow crevices in sunny quarters is the dear old wood sorrel. It has tiny leaves like a shamrock in shape, but of a warm red-brown colour, and the sweetest little yellow flowers imaginable; they are borne on very short stalks, and only come out when the sunshine encourages them; the whole plant does not exceed three inches in height; it spreads rapidly, seeds freely, and thrives best in a very light soil; it will also do well on walls.

The alpine poppies are so delicate and graceful that they seem made for the rockery. They only grow six inches high, and continue in flower at least four months; they may be had in a great range of colours, and are easily brought up from seed. Nice bushy plants can be had of these poppies for about four shillings a dozen, and it is needless to say they require plenty of sunshine. The word phlox conveys to many people the idea of a tall autumn-flowering plant, with large umbels of flowers, individually about the size of a shilling. But these are not the only species; the alpine varieties are just as beautiful in a different way, though some are not more than a few inches high, and each flower no bigger than a ladies' glove button. In spring and early summer they become perfect sheets of bloom, so that the foliage is completely hidden; when out of flower, they are soft green cushions of plants, and serve to cover bare bricks well.

The alpine potentillas are pretty, and keep in flower for a long time. *P. nepalensis* is a good one, but the merits of *P. fruticosa* are much exaggerated, its dirty-looking yellow flowers are by no means prepossessing.

No rockery is complete without several specimens of the family of saxifrages. One cannot do better than make a beginning with them, as they are so fine in form and diverse in style. *S. aizoon compactum* is one of the best rosette species, and *S. hypnoides densa* of the mossy tribe; other kinds well worth growing are *S. burseriana*, which has pretty white flowers on red hairy stems in early March; *S. cunifolia*, with charming fresh pink blossoms, and of course *S. umbrosa*, the sweet old-fashioned London pride. A dry sunny situation suits the saxifrages best.

The houseleeks are somewhat similar in appearance, but like drier situations than the last named plants. The sempervivums delight to creep along a piece of bare rock, and one marvels how they can derive enough sustenance from the small amount of poor soil in which they are often seen growing. The cobweb species, called *arachnoideum*, is most interesting, and invariably admired by visitors; it has greyish-green rosettes, each one of which is covered with a downy thread in the form of a spider's web. A kind more often seen is *sempervivum montanum*, and certainly it is a very handsome species, with curious flowers supported on firm succulent red stems. It is to be seen in broad clumps at Kew, and very well it looks.

There are no better carpetters than the dwarf sedums, or stonecrops. *Sedum glaucum* has blue-grey foliage, and spreads rapidly; *S. lydium* is the variety most in use, and can be had very cheaply. The tall, old variety, *sedum spectabile*, has been improved upon, and the novelty is called *S. s. rosea*. Another novelty is shortia galacifolia; it is a native of North America, and has white, bell-shaped flowers supported on elegant, hairy stems, the leaves are heart shaped, and turn almost scarlet in autumn; thus, the plant has two seasons of beauty, as it blooms in the spring. A peaty soil, with a little sand added, suits it well, if the drainage is good; and it likes a half-shady position.

Plants that are sadly neglected are the airy-fairy Sea lavenders or Statices, with their filmy heads like purple foam; *S. gmelini* and *S. limonium* are two of the best. When cut, they last a long time, and are very useful for giving a graceful appearance to stiff bouquets.

The dwarf thalictrums are good rockery plants;

they are grown for their foliage, which bears a striking resemblance to the maidenhair fern. *T. adiantifolium* and *T. minus* are very pretty; their flower-heads should always be cut off, so as to promote the production of their fine fronds, which have the property of lasting well when cut.

The aromatic scent of thyme is very pleasant on a rockery; not only should the silver and golden varieties be grown, but also those bright kinds which give us sheets of purple, pink, and white blossom during summer; to thrive they must be exposed to full sunshine, when they will attract innumerable bees. The new kind, *T. serpyllum roseus*, is splendid, the tiny flowers coming in such profusion as to completely hide the foliage. All are low-growing, having the cushion habit of growth.

Veronicas are not often seen, yet they are exceedingly pretty, and continuous bloomers. Amateurs should not begin with the shrub tribe, as these are somewhat tender, but if *V. incana*, *V. longifolia-subsessilis*, and *V. prostrata* are obtained, they will be sure to please. The first and last are low growing, but the other is two feet high, and has long racenes like soft blue tassels, which hang down in the most charming way.

A few words on some more bulbs that look well on rockeries, besides the crocus and dwarf iris before-mentioned, may not be amiss: the winter aconites are most appropriate so placed, and show to greater advantage than in the level border. Their golden flowers, each surrounded by a frill of green, come forth as early as January, if the weather be propitious.

The chionodoxa, called also glory of the snow, is very fresh and pretty, with its bright blue flowers having a conspicuous white eye. If left undisturbed they will spread rapidly, and come up year after year without any further trouble; they are very cheap, and will do in any soil.

Snowdrops are charming on rockwork, and may be placed close to the chionodoxa, as they bloom almost together.

The grape hyacinths have very quaint little flowers of a bright dark-blue colour, on stalks about five or six inches high; they flower for some weeks, and must be massed together to get a good effect.

The early-flowering scillas resemble the chionodoxas, but last much longer in bloom. They are very easy to manage, and rarely fail to make a good show. *S. siberica* is the best-known variety, and can be obtained very cheaply.

The miniature narcissus is the sweetest thing imaginable; *N. minus*, is only a few inches high, and when in the open border is apt to get splashed, but amongst stones in a sheltered position on the rockery they are charming. All these dwarf bulbs look so well in such positions, because their purity remains unsullied.

Here I will leave the rockery, merely intimating that early autumn is the best time for planting, and that if pains are taken to construct it properly at first, a great amount of trouble will be saved in the end. Most of these plants and bulbs may be had of Messrs. Barr & Sons, 12 King Street, Covent Garden. Their daffodil nurseries at Long Ditton, near Surbiton, Surrey, are famous all the world over, but they also go in a great deal for hardy perennials and rock plants, of which they have a splendid stock; their prices are very reasonable, too, when you take into consideration that everything they send out is absolutely true to name. Their interesting catalogues will be sent post free on application.

CHAPTER 10

Trees, Shrubs, and How to Treat Them

Some good plants for growing beneath them ~ Selection of hardy shrubs ~ Enriching the soil ~ Climbers.

Forest trees in a small garden are somewhat out of place, but as they are often found in such positions, I will deal with them here. It is to be remembered that though they give most grateful shade, not only do they rob everything beneath them of sunshine, but also take so much out of the soil, that, unless constant renewals are made, very little can be grown in their immediate vicinity; the class of plants that will do best beneath their branches also find the soil they are growing in best renewed by the leaves which fall therefrom. For the sake of tidiness, these of course are swept away, but they should be kept for two or three years, and then brought back, converted into leaf mould; if this is not done, the quality of the soil will steadily deteriorate, instead of getting richer, as it does in woods; and this is one reason why so many wild plants fail to thrive when brought into cultivation; manure is no substitute, but often distasteful to them.

Something besides ivy

Trees must be divided into two broad sections, deciduous and evergreen. Very few plants will do well under the latter, but as regards the first, ivy is not by any means the only thing that will grow, though it is often a good plan to use it as a foundation, and work in plants here and there afterwards. There is no need to choose the large kind; those elegant varieties with long pointed leaves are more ornamental and just as easy to grow. Their roots must be restricted when other plants are near, or they will soon take up all the room. Ferns will do very well under trees, if they are plentifully watered during the dry season. Here also a few of the choicest kinds should be grown, for though some of them may not do so well as in a shady open spot, most of them will give a fairly good account of themselves. Always plant them with the rhizome above ground, not forgetting that when each fern has its full complement of fronds, it will take up a considerably larger space than it does at the time it is set out.

If the *Osmunda regalis* is tried – the royal fern – it is necessary to get a good established turf of it; strong clumps cost about 1 shilling 6 pence each; plenty of water must be given it in the summer. I have seen it in splendid form under a tree in a very small garden.

Perhaps the St. John's worts come next to ivy and

ferns in their usefulness for planting under trees, as they are always decorative, being evergreen. In the spring, the foliage is a most lovely soft apple-green, and in summer when the golden cups filled with anthers issue forth from the axils of the leaves, the effect is beautiful. *Hypericum calycinum* is the Latin term for these plants, and though they will do on the dryest bank and in the poorest soil, being very tough and wiry, if they are grown in good loam and manure is occasionally given them, they will repay with far finer flowers, which will be produced for a longer season.

A good breadth of woodruff makes a very pretty picture for several weeks, and has a delightful scent; here and there bulbs can be planted amongst it, neither being harmed by this plan. The aubrietias flower with unfailing regularity under trees, even when the aspect is north, and no gleam of sunshine reaches them; their greyish-green rosettes resist drought splendidly, and though these plants do not give us so much blossom in unfavourable positions, still they make a very pretty show. Aubrietias can be easily propagated by division; every morsel grows.

Banks under trees

The white arabis also does well under similar conditions; both are useful for draping perpendicular surfaces, such as the steep side of a bank or hedge. A raised border, with facing of bricks, is rather a nice way of growing plants under trees, and the work of tending them is pleasant, less stooping being required.

The mossy saxifrage droops over the edges, and mingles well with the arabis, but it must be more carefully watered, as it is apt to die out; pieces should constantly be taken off, and dibbled in so as to fill up any gaps. The periwinkles meander charmingly over the roughest stones, and in the most dreary spots; their glossy evergreen leaves, and fresh bright little flowerets always looking cheerful whatever the weather. They creep quickly, rooting every few inches as they grow; on the perpendicular face of the rock, succulent plants like echeverias can sometimes be made to grow (those little green rosettes, having each leaf tipped with red, which can be bought so readily in May for about twopence each).

Many things will do for a time, that want renewing each year, even if hardy. Cowslips, primroses, polyanthus, wallflowers, all will make a fair show if planted out just before flowering, but, unless a few hours' sun daily shines on them, they will not retain enough vitality to produce seed, and being biennial soon die out, leaving not a trace behind.

A great many bulbs do admirably under deciduous trees, especially those which blossom before the new leaves on the branches above them have reached any appreciable size.

Scillas bloom in the same place year after year; snowdrops also do fairly well, and lilies of the valley ring out a few of their dainty bells every spring (a rich vegetable soil suits them best). Tulips only do well when planted afresh every autumn; but, as they are so cheap, that is not a great matter. The megaseas, mentioned in another chapter, give forth many of their fine leaves, but they refuse to turn colour, owing to the want of sun. Foxgloves, also, grow and flower, seeming to enjoy their position.

If the aspect of the space to be filled is a cold one, such things as geraniums will only give a few poor flowers, and then succumb. Even pansies wilt and gradually fade away under trees, for their soft, weak stems and leaves soon get drawn up for want of light, though they will do well enough on an open border, facing north.

Hardwooded plants will be generally found to do best; indeed, some of the shrub tribe succeed very well, particularly barberry, pernettyas, the early daphnes, whortleberries, *Gaultheria shallon* and cotoneaster.

While on the subject of shrubs, it may be as well to mention several attractive kinds which may be planted in place of the eternal box and Portugal laurel; of course, these two have almost every good quality; they will do in any soil, are evergreen, and resist smoke, dust and dirt well; but, in places where poor soil and a soot-laden atmosphere are absent, substitutes might occasionally be found for those shrubs, which will have the added charm of novelty. One of the nicest for small gardens is *cotoneaster microphylla*; this is a joy to look at, all through the winter months, when it is at its best; the branches grow in an uncommon manner, and are of somewhat prostrate habit; they are thickly clothed with dark, small leaves the whole way up the stem, and shining amongst them are the pretty crimson, almost transparent berries. It is quite distinct from the ordinary berry-bearing shrubs, as there is nothing stiff about its gracefully-curving sprays, which look well cut and wedged in the Japanese fashion. Shrubs of this variety may be had as low as sixpence, but it is better policy to get a larger one, costing about eighteen pence, as they will sooner be of a presentable size; they are shrubs, too, that do not altogether show their capabilities when at a very youthful stage.

A good all round plant

Berberis aquifolium is another shrub which has a great deal to recommend it; it is evergreen, and will do in almost any position; it bears lovely yellow flowers in spring, purple powdered berries in August, and the foliage turns a rich red in October. Always ornate, it is one of the easiest shrubs to grow, and just the thing for a small garden.

The myrtle, though liable to be killed in a very hard frost, can often be grown to a great size in a sheltered garden; I have seen bushes eight yards round, in an exposed position near the river Thames, which must have been braving the storms for many a year past. They should not be planted out till March or April, though November is the month for most other shrubs. The old *pyrus japonica* makes a good bush, though most often grow on a wall; its bright flowers, carmine-scarlet in colour with yellow anthers in the centre, appear early in April, a week or two later than the climbers, which of course are protected. When grown in bush form, it is sometimes pruned out of all recognition; this is especially the case in public gardens, and is quite an affliction to any one who knows how lovely it can be! The knife should be restrained, allowing the pyrus to take its own shape as much as possible; it is often sold under the name of *cydonia japonica*, as that is really its rightful title.

One or two of the araucarias make very good shrubs for a small garden; they should not be grown in cold, windswept places, as their branches soon turn brown if exposed to continued frost and furious blasts. There is a magnificent specimen in the nurseries of

Messrs. Veitch, Kingston Hill, Surrey, planted about 1865; its ornamental appearance is greatly due to the number of young branches springing out from the main trunk and almost completely covering it; they nestle under the larger branches, and produce a very picturesque effect. Small plants of this variety may be had for three or four shillings.

Messrs. Veitch have a splendid selection of shrubs, all in the best of health; their hollies are well grown, and include all the good sorts; a variety that bears fruit when quite young is *ilex glabrum*, of which they have a large stock; these trees are such slow growers, that it is advisable to get one that will look attractive almost at once.

Pernettyas are ornamental little shrubs, not so much grown as they deserve; in winter, when most things look drooping and unhappy, these American visitors to our gardens are bright and cheerful. The dwarf *Erica carnea*, both pink and white, show their buds as early as November, and at the turn of the year present a very pretty appearance; they look well as edgings to rhododendron beds; their price is about sixpence each.

Another charming winter shrub is *cornus sanguinea*; its beauty lies in the red glow of its leafless stems, which makes it visible some distance off.

Spirea Anthony Waterer is a fine plant in late summer, having pink umbels of flowers and a habit somewhat like the valerian. The snowberry is good in autumn and winter, having large white berries which hang on a long time; it is deciduous, and likes a rich soil.

Messrs. Veitch have a splendid collection of conifers for all aspects and positions; their small junipers are most fascinating little trees, with flat spreading branches of the loveliest shade of green, and their seedling firs are well balanced. They sell a great variety of lilac trees too.

Grafted lilacs

A note on lilacs will not be amiss; if you notice that any lilacs you may happen to have flower sparsely, and are poor in size and colour it will be as well to examine the stems close to the soil, and you will probably find a fine crop of suckers; all these must be cut away as sedulously as those on your rose trees, for nearly all lilacs are grafted, very few kinds being sold on their own roots.

The forsythias are pretty climbers or shrubs, according to the variety chosen, much like the yellow jasmine, with its golden stars on leafless stems. Just as the latter, however, is going out of flower the forsythias are coming on, and therefore give a succession of very pretty blossoms.

Originally from China, the wigelias have now taken a place in many English gardens, by reason of their fresh pink and white flowers and easy cultivation. They bloom late in spring, and should be placed by preference against a dark wall, as their flowers, being surrounded by pale-green foliage, do not stand out sufficiently on a light one.

The delicate Ceanothus

The exquisite summer-flowering ceanothus has been mentioned before, but I notice it here again because it is one of those shrubs that should not be overlooked on any account; its leaves are somewhat like those of a heliotrope, and its flowers are bluish-mauve in colour and borne in trusses; it blooms for many weeks and has a most delicious scent, and should be planted out in the spring.

A neglected but really remarkable shrub is the *rhus cotinus* – the smoke plant. In early August it is a striking sight, with its curious inflorescence quite impossible to describe. At Hampton Court there are two or three fine species.

Winter shrubbery

It will be observed that shrubs presenting a decorative appearance in winter are made much of; this is because softwooded plants always look miserable then, whereas with a few berry-bearing shrubs and a nice selection of bulbs, we may have a pretty garden all the year round. Once planted, however, they should not be left entirely to take care of themselves; the soil must be enriched occasionally, if we wish for good results, and great care taken to train them in the way they should go, by pinching out shoots which would tend to give a lopsided effect. Such things as firs must be unobtrusively staked till they are able to support themselves, as symmetrical growth is part of their charm, and we must remember that 'as the twig is bent, the tree is inclined'. Standard rhododendrons require to be very carefully staked until they have a fair hold of the ground, or their big heads are caught by the wind, and this loosens the soil to such an extent that it is impossible for fresh roots to be made. Generally, some of the bush rhododendrons should be grown amongst the standards, and if these are dotted about with clumps of lilies the effect is very rich. *Lilium tigrinum splendens* is one of the best for this purpose, and is most brilliantly beautiful during August and September; they are six feet in height, and the flowers are a rich orange red, with black spots on each petal; they can be obtained for half-a-crown the dozen.

A lily suitable for placing amongst azaleas, as it is only three feet high, is *lilium speciosum album*; it has glistening pure-white flowers, and a graceful habit. The shade of the shrub is most beneficial to the lilies, as they dislike strong sunshine, and of course they are also protected from cold in winter. The same soil, a mixture of peat, loam and sand, suits both.

CHAPTER II

The Ins and Outs of Gardening

Planting ~ Watering ~ 'Puddling' ~ Aspect ~ Shelter ~ Youth and age in relation to plants ~ Catalogue defects ~ A time for everything.

Now that we have seen what to plant, it will be advisable to learn how to plant it.

Perhaps the most important point to be taken notice of is the necessity of firm planting. Watch how a clever gardener presses the earth well round the roots of everything he puts in, where the plants are large, treading the soil down with his foot. Loose planting is ruinous (except in a few isolated cases), and yet it is a favourite practice with amateurs, who call it treating their flowers tenderly! But, as with the human kind, a judicious mixture of firmness and tenderness is the happy medium to be aimed at, and which alone insures success.

A good watering helps to make the soil settle as much as anything; therefore, when put into the ground the plants should be well soaked, after which they should be left for a few days, with the exception of overhead watering, which is most refreshing. In very hot weather, it is often possible to transplant with perfect safety, if the roots are put into 'puddle'.

Planting in 'Puddle'

'Puddle' is a very expressive gardening term, which signifies soil mixed with so much water as almost to have acquired the consistency of a paste.

Operation 1 – well water the plant to be removed; *operation 2* – dig the hole which is to receive it; *operation 3* – fill the same with water up to the rim; *operation 4* – carefully take up your plant with plenty of soil round it; *operation 5* – gently place it in hole prepared, the walls of which will then be thoroughly soaked; *operation 6* – fill in with the 'puddle' above referred to; *operation 7* – tread gently but firmly down; and, lastly, scatter a little dryer soil on the top. Flowers planted in this fashion can be taken up even during June, July and August; and, if properly looked after, will scarcely flag at all.

Effects of aspect

The influence of aspect on plants is an interesting study; we all know that a shrub on a south wall is practically in a different climate to a shrub on a north wall. One reason why tender plants do so well on a south or west aspect is because the sun does not reach it till some hours after it has risen and warmed the air. The sun shining on half-frozen buds often has a disastrous effect on plants climbing walls with an eastern aspect; consequently, a north wall is often better for a delicate plant, if the warmest aspect cannot be given it; camellias, for instance, when outside prefer it to any other. If a succession of one kind of flower is desired, a group facing each corner of the compass will often accomplish this, sometimes as much difference as a month being noted. Certain unimpressionable plants refuse to alter their season of blooming, but, as a rule, it is a sure method of attaining this object. Colouring is also vastly influenced by aspect; such things as pansies, for example, never show such rich markings under a hot sun, but require an east border to bring out their true beauties. Scotland suits them admirably, with its cool summer nights and moist atmosphere.

The importance of shelter

Shelter has a great deal to do with success in a garden; in the ordinary town garden, the builder has generally been only too obliging in this respect, but in bleak hilly spots it might almost be called the gardener's watchword. Few things except Scotch firs and the like will stand a long-continued high wind with impunity; not only does it wrench the plants out of the soil, but, if it comes from a cold quarter, both flowers and leaves curl up at its approach and refuse to thrive; they become nipped in the bud, as at the touch of frost. Everyone has experienced the meaning of shelter when out in a cold nor'easter; how it bites one, making the blood stand still with its fury! then, all at once, we round the corner, and hey presto! all is changed; the air is quite caressing, and the blood tingles to our very fingertips from the sudden reaction. With due regard to shelter, then, climates can be 'manufactured' without glass. In extensive grounds, these windbreaks are made by planting lines of trees, but in smaller spaces it may be done differently. The construction of light fences, not over five feet in height, run up inside the compound, accomplish a good deal, as may be seen by any visitor to the nurseries of Messrs. Barr, at Long Ditton; they are not ugly if well clothed, and make an effectual break in a much shorter time than would be the case if fruit trees were planted, though there is nothing prettier than a row of apple or pear trees, grown espalier fashion, if time is no object. Many things will nestle beneath them, and flower beautifully for months together, for, though these fruit trees are deciduous, the force of the wind is considerably lessened by them, on the same principle that fishing nets are such a protection from frost to wall climbers; and this again may be compared to the veils which ladies use to protect their skin. Though of wide mesh, the fishing nets will keep off five or six degrees of frost, and in certain cases are better than a closer protection, like tiffany, which sometimes 'coddles' the trees too much.

A few words on the respective qualities of youth and age may not be amiss. Amateurs are so often disappointed in their garden purchases, because they will not allow the plants sufficient time to demonstrate their capabilities. Catalogues are much to blame in this respect; an enticing description of a shrub is given, and the confiding amateur orders it, believing that in a year or two it will fulfil its character. How can he be expected to know that that particular variety never bears any flowers worth speaking of till it is at least seven years old! In the long run, I think nurserymen will find it pay to tell the whole truth regarding each plant they send out, not merely in a negative way either. If an alpine, for example, like *Linnea borealis*, is extremely difficult to grow and flower in this country, it is only fair to say so; to place it amongst a lot of easily-cultivated plants without a word of warning is not straightforward dealing, moreover is apt to make people disgusted with the whole thing. Some plants bloom much the best when in their first youth; this is the case with many of the softwooded plants, which soon give signs of exhaustion, especially in a light soil. When it is noticed that the outside flowering stems produce finer blossoms than those from the centre, it is generally a sign that division is required, and that the soil wants enriching.

The calendar

That there is a time for everything in gardening is almost a truism; the calendar is considered one of the most important parts of a technical book on this subject. It is advisable for an amateur gardener to have a notebook, in which he jots down what he has to do several weeks or months in advance; so often some fault easily remedied is left over from year to year, because perhaps it is only observed in the summer, and cannot be mended till winter. Recently, the calendar has not been given quite so much prominence; gardeners find out more and more that the weather is not governed by it, and that though one year it may be best to sow a certain seed at the beginning of February, another season may be so cold that it will have to go in at least a fortnight later. Nevertheless, taken roughly, this diary of events, as the dictionary calls it, holds good for most years, and it is wise to stick to it as far as possible.

CHAPTER 12

The Profitable Portion

Fruit ~ The best kinds for a small garden ~ Avoidance of size minus flavour ~ Vegetables ~ Herbs.

If a small garden has room for any fruit trees, apples are the most useful kind to grow; they can be so trained as to take up little room; for instance, in espalier fashion, down each side of a sunny walk. These apple hedges are a lovely sight in spring and also in the autumn, when the ruddy fruit is waiting to drop into the outstretched hand. Though names can easily be given, it is generally a good plan to make enquiries in the neighbourhood as to the best varieties to grow, for so much depends on soil and position. Colloquial names are often given, which require identifying with existing varieties; this can be done by sending up a specimen of the fruit to the manager of a correspondence column in some reliable gardening magazine. These gentlemen are generally able to give the desired information, and no charge is made. A surer method still is to send the fruit which it is desired to identify to some well-known nurseries, such as those of Messrs. Rivers at Sawbridgeworth, Hertfordshire; they have acres upon acres of splendid fruit trees of every kind, and my readers cannot do better than purchase all they require from them. Having such wide experience, they can recommend varieties suitable for all kinds of soil and all sorts of positions. For small gardens, apple trees grafted on the paradise stock are much to be recommended, as they are compact in habit, taking up but little room and begin bearing almost at once. Messrs. Rivers guarantee their trees on this stock to continue in full bearing for many years. 'Plant pears, and you plant for your heirs' is the old saying, but this is all changed now that the quince stock is used so much. Cordon pears on wire fencing bear first rate crops, and are particularly good for small gardens; the diagonal cordon is perhaps the best. Cooking pears can be grown on north walls, but it is not advisable to try dessert varieties on such a cold aspect.

Stone fruit

To grow stone fruit successfully, the soil must contain a fair quantity of lime; moreover the trees, especially if trained against walls, must be kept well watered at the stoning period. After the fruit has been picked, less moisture is required.

Standard plants are very profitable, as crops of

currants and gooseberries can be grown beneath them; this double system of cropping the ground being a great advantage where space is a consideration. Plums require little pruning, and are also not so liable to attacks of birds as other fruit. When ordering, do not get too many trees of one variety, a good selection will give a long succession of fruit; this applies to all kinds of fruit trees.

Currants are a very manageable fruit, as they do well in almost any position; heavy crops can be secured from bushes planted on north borders, the black currant thriving though it only gets a minimum of sunshine; gooseberries are not exacting either, and will give a good return for a small amount of labour. Both may be propagated by cuttings, and are very reasonable in price, only costing about four shillings a dozen. Messrs. Rivers' stock of maiden peach trees and nectarines is unsurpassed, and many of the best kinds obtainable have been raised by them, and are of worldwide fame. Regarding that oft-debated question of protecting the blossom in spring, they do not advise anything in the nature of bracken to be used, this often doing more harm than good. If possible, a glass coping should be placed along the top of the wall, from which tiffany can depend on cold nights; unless this be done, it is best to leave them alone. Fine crops are often obtained in the south and west of England without any protection whatever, the good seasons amply compensating for the bad.

It occasionally happens that the amateur has an advantage over the market grower. This is particularly the case where one wants to curtail the depredations of birds; it pays to protect a few yards of fruit, but where it is a case of several acres, the trees have to take their chance. Cherries have to be watched very carefully in this respect; it is very desirable to keep the Morello cherries hanging long, as they then become sweeter and make good tarts. These trees do very well on north walls.

Want of flavour

One great fault noticeable in fruit growing of recent years is that everything is sacrificed to size and appearance, flavour being at a discount; the shows have had a great deal to do with this; in the old days, when they were fewer in number, the test of a fruit was its taste. Strawberries in particular have deteriorated in this way, the huge kinds now seen often being absolutely devoid of the luscious flavour generally associated with them. Of course we have better keeping varieties, and they can be obtained much later than was once the case. If the culture of the perpetual varieties is extended strawberries will be in season many weeks longer, and this will be extremely good news for invalids, who find it as a rule one of the easiest fruits to digest. The cultivation of strawberries is fairly easy, but their wants must be regularly attended to. Once in three years the old plants must be taken up, and new ones (the 'runners' issuing from the old) planted instead; in the summer a good mulching of strawy manure should be placed between the rows, as this helps to keep the fruit clean, besides enriching the soil. Plants which are expected to bear a good crop of fruit must have all their runners cut off as fast as they appear, as it exhausts the plants much to bear both. Strawberries are partial to rather a light soil, but nearly all other fruit trees revel in a mixture of loam and clay, with a little sand to keep it open. This soil does not suffer so much from drought, and, being firmer, the larger trees can send their roots down and get a far better hold of the ground than is possible in shingly, poor soils.

Ornamental and useful

Vegetables take up a good deal of room in a garden if they are wanted all the year round, but a few things can be easily grown. Scarlet runner beans, being ornamental as well as useful, are some of the best vegetables to grow, as they can be made to form a convenient screen for a rubbish heap. These can be brought up from seed sown early in April, and, when a foot high, require sticks; these come rather expensive if new ones are used every summer, but with care they will last two and even three seasons, though latterly they become very brittle. On the rubbish heap, marrows can be grown with the greatest facility, as they revel in the rich warmth there found. They should be bought when a few inches high, and planted out at the end of May, as they are only half hardy. When the flower at the end drops off they are ready to cut; if allowed to get much larger they lose all their flavour. A few, however, should be allowed to become quite ripe, as they can be used in the autumn for making apple tart, two parts apple to one part marrow, and they also make a good jam when spiced with ginger, etc.

Relations of the sunflowers

Jerusalem artichokes will flourish on a north border, and come in very nicely during November; they are planted in exactly the same manner as potatoes, that is, by means of pieces containing two or three 'eyes', which should go in about February. Like potatoes, too, they can be stored; though so tall, they do not require any sticks; these artichokes present much the same appearance as the ordinary cottager's sunflower (indeed, the botanical name is identical, *helianthus*), having thick, hollow stems, covered with long, pointed, hairy leaves.

Potatoes are rather 'kittle-kattle' for amateurs, but where the soil is light they should certainly be tried, especially where there is room for a rotation of crops, as successive planting should not be made in the same place. Beware of giving rank manure to them, a sure precursor of disease; artificial manures, such as guano are far more suitable. No trees must be allowed near them, but a sunny open piece of ground be given up to them. March is the month to plant and the rows should be from fifteen inches to two feet apart.

Carrots and turnips also prefer a light soil and sunny situation. Seeds of both should be sown in March, when the soil is in a friable condition, several times subsequently; the seeds must be well thinned out, and the space between the rows constantly turned by the hoe; the latter operation is particularly needful in heavy land, as it not only destroys weeds, but prevents the soil from caking: the rows should be about a foot apart. Before the turnips are ready, the young green tops make a vegetable by no means to be despised.

Herbs, such as mint, parsley, mustard and cress,

should be grown in every garden, as they take up but little space and are so much dearer to buy. Mint is perennial, and will come up year after year, giving no trouble whatever; it spreads rapidly and will grow anywhere. To start a bed, roots can be bought from some market gardener, or cuttings can be struck from the bunches bought in the shops.

Parsley is a biennial, though generally grown as an annual, because the leaves from young plants are much the best; the seeds should be sown two or three times a year, beginning about February, in a sheltered nook; this herb likes plenty of sun; even the curliest varieties degenerate if placed in a damp shady situation. It prefers light soil, and gives a better winter supply than where the soil is heavy. Flowerheads must be cut off regularly to keep the plants in good condition, though just a few of the best kinds may be allowed to perfect their seed, which should be sown as soon as ripe. Mustard and cress should also be sown several times during the summer; the cress must be sown three or four days before the mustard, to obtain them ready for cutting at the same time; both must be cut almost directly they appear, as, if allowed to grow tall, they become tough, and their flavour is lost; these seeds require no thinning out, the exception that proves the rule.

CHAPTER 13

Annuals and Biennials

How to grow annuals ~ Some good kinds ~ Some good biennials.

Many amateurs look upon annuals as rubbishy things to grow, and only suitable for the children's gardens, but that is because they have generally failed to grow them properly. With the improved kinds now in cultivation, it is possible to make the portion of the flower garden devoted to them 'a thing of beauty' if not 'a joy forever'. As it is more satisfactory to bring them up from the beginning, I have described in Chapter 16, a method generally successful. Seed-sowing out-of-doors being rather precarious, I have found it advisable to sow all the smaller seeds either in a greenhouse or frame, however hardy the annual be. This not only saves endless trouble in the way of protecting the seed from birds, etc., but is advantageous in that one has an earlier display of bloom, owing to the growth being quicker under glass. Below is a table of the choicest kinds:

Annuals
(name, length, colour)

Bartonia aurea (1 to 1½ ft.) – Golden yellow.

Celosia plumosa (1½ ft.) – Red and yellow.
Somewhat after the style of Prince's feather; tender

Coreopsis, or *Calliopsis* (2 ft.) – Yellow and red

Eschscholtzia (1 ft.) – Bright yellow
Very pretty grey-green foliage; select

Gaillardia (1½ ft.) – Yellow and red
The 'blanket flower'; good for cutting

Godetia (9 ins.) – Red to white
Cup-shaped; showy

Mesembryanthemum (½ to 1 ft.) – Ice plant.
Grown for its foliage, which glistens
beautifully; must have sun

Ionopsidium acaule (2 to 3 ins.) – Pale mauve.
Miniature plants for filling up crevices in rockwork

Linum coccineum (1 ft.) – New scarlet variety

Lupinus arboreus 'Snow queen' (3 to 4 ft.) – Pure white ~ A very stately plant; new

Nemophila grandiflora (½ ft.) – Beautiful blue and white ~ Remind one of the eyes of a child

Phlox drummondi (1 ft.) – All shades of red to white Half-hardy; must be massed

Shirley poppy (1 ft.) – All shades of pink Very graceful and free; light soil

Portulaca (½ ft.) – Mixed colours The most effective of all annuals; half-hardy; must have plenty of sun and a light soil

Salpiglossis (1½ ft.) – All shades Very fragile flowers, veined and marked in exquisite fashion; must be massed

Silene pendula compacta (½ ft.) – Bright pink Flowers shaped somewhat like a Maltese cross

Stocks, double, ten week (1 ft.) – Various When thinning, only keep the weakest seedlings, as those are the double ones

BIENNIALS

These, if sown one spring, will not flower
the following summer, but do so the year after.

Foxgloves (3 to 4 ft.) – White and coloured
White, most picturesque; all do well in shade;
unless seed is required, cut out main stem,
when side shoots will flower

Lunaria biennis (1½ to 2 ft.) – The old 'honesty'
Much prized for its silvery seedpods

Polyanthus (½ ft.) – Mixed colours
Admirable for shady places; water well

Japanese pinks (1 ft.) – Deepest crimson to white
Fringed petals; a whole bed of this is lovely

Sweet Williams (1 ft.) – Mixed shades
Auricula type, the best; there is a novelty,
blackish-maroon in shade, which should be placed
amongst some of the crimson varieties

Snapdragons (2 ft.) – Varied
Flower from June to November;
eschew reds of a mauve hue

Wallflower, 'Ruby Gem' (2 ft.) – Reddish violet

The seeds of all these, true to name and ripe for germination, may be obtained from Messrs. Barr, Long Ditton, Surrey, who sell sixpenny packets of all these kinds; small quantities of the well-known sorts only costing threepence. This is a great advantage to owners of small gardens, as one does not wish to give 1 shilling 6 pence or 2 shillings 6 pence for perhaps two thousand seeds of one variety, when only two or three dozen are required. Penny packets of seeds may be had from the One and All Company at most greengrocer's, and are really wonderful value for the money.

CHAPTER 14

Window Boxes

How to make them ~ Relation of box to residence they are intended to adorn ~ Suitable soil ~ Window plants for different aspects.

Where gardens are small, one seems to need window boxes more than where there is land and to spare. They add to the number of one's flowers, and, if carefully looked after, decidedly improve the appearance of a house. That is a large 'If' though, for unkempt boxes only make it look untidy.

Flowers first, box second

Though the tiled sort obtain a good deal of patronage, nothing really looks much better than boxes covered with virgin cork, if constantly renewed, for it acts as a foil to the flowers, whereas patterned tiles are rather apt to take one's attention away from them. In summer, certainly, they have the advantage of preserving the earth in a moist condition, and in smoky towns they help to give a bright, clean look to the houses so decorated. Old-fashioned houses, however, should always have their window boxes made in the virgin cork style, as they accord better with their surroundings.

When strong wooden boxes have been procured, it is quite easy to tack on the cork one's self, provided one has a sharp knife and a good supply of long nails, and it is most fascinating work; it is advisable to wear gloves during the process, as the hands may become rough otherwise. Seven pounds of the cork may be had for a shilling of any seedsman, and three lots will do two boxes of the average size. The soil should be fairly light, like that used for potting, but before the boxes are filled, several holes, bored with a red-hot poker, should be made in the bottom, and a thin layer of 'crocks' spread over them; do not quite fill the box with soil, but leave an inch or two free to allow of watering, and even more if a layer of moss or cocoanut fibre is used to cover the surface of the soil; this is certainly an improvement till the plants get large enough to cover it themselves. Only artificial manures must be used to fertilize the roots, and even those must not be given too often, but only in the hot weather, when growth is quick, as they are stimulating to a great degree.

Constant renewals are necessary, if the boxes are to look gay all the year round; even the best gardeners acknowledge this. If continuous bloomers are chosen, however, the cost is considerably modified. Perhaps the winter shrubs are the most expensive item; yet they are often chosen without much regard to cheerfulness; indeed, the favourite kinds present a most funereal appearance.

Aspect has always a good deal to do with the selection of plants, but in the case of windows facing north and east, it is the cold winds more than the absence of sun which restricts the choice. Shelter is a great factor in their wellbeing.

Showy in winter

In a cosy box with a western exposure, and protected on the north, the golden-tipped retinosporas make a pretty show during the cold months of the year, and form a welcome change from the prevailing dark green tones. Cotoneasters, pernettyas, and the variegated euonymus are also very suitable. The polypody ferns, being evergreen, look very well too, and will thrive facing all four points of the compass. In the spring, dwarf wallflowers, interspersed with different kinds of bulbs, make the boxes look bright, and the new *pyrus maulei* is also very pretty at this season. The perennial candytuft, too, is a splendid flower for late spring, particularly *Iberis correafolia*, which has a neat habit, and bears quantities of snow-white flowers; it likes sun, and not too much moisture. The yellow jasmine, which is so pretty in winter, looks extremely well when allowed to droop over the edges of a box, as it flowers in quite a young state. The mossy saxifrages are suitable for the edges of the box, and are always ornamental; their charming white flowers, supported on red stalks, appear about May.

Such bulbs as the Duc Van Thol tulips are very bright, and mix well with the shrubs; they should be put in some time in October. Crocuses look well, too, but should not be placed in the same box as the tulips, or too gaudy an appearance will result. A thick planting along the front of the box of the Starch hyacinth – *muscari* – is uncommon, and an exceedingly nice thing to have, as the moment the window is open fragrant whiffs, resembling new-mown hay, pour into the room, especially on a sunny morning. When these bulbs have to make way for the summer flowers, it is advisable to plant them out in the garden and use another lot next year, as the constant transplantation somewhat weakens them. Of course, one could leave them in the box during the summer, if it were not for the unsightly decaying leaves, which must on no account be cut off.

About the middle of May for the South of England, and a fortnight later for the North, is the time to furnish the boxes for the summer. If the window is small, low growing plants and trailers should prevail.

For cold aspects

Some good flowers for north and east aspects are fuchsias, calceolarias, begonias, and the lovely white *campanula isophylla*; the latter thrives best in such conditions, bearing finer flowers for a much greater length of time than where the sun scorches it. These plants accord well with stucco, which serves to show up their whiteness more than anything. Marguerites, yellow and white, also thrive in the cooler windows of a house, and are not so exigent in the matter of watering when so placed. When selecting begonias for boxes it is well to choose the single varieties with moderate-sized blossoms; the big flabby ones soon become spoilt by rain, and are not produced so freely, nor is their habit of growth so good.

For hot situations the double geraniums are splendid, but they should not be mixed with lobelias, as they look infinitely better when grouped by themselves, the shades ranging from dark crimson to the palest salmon-pink.

Pretty trailers

The quick-growing tradescantia with its many-jointed stems and glossy bright green leaves, softens the somewhat formal appearance of the geraniums, and will cover all the bare soil in a marvellously short space of time, and droop over the edges in long streamers; it is quite distinct from the tall tradescantias mentioned in a former chapter, and is the easiest thing in the world to propagate, as any little bits saved over from a bouquet will make roots in a bowl of water, or they can be 'struck' in the ordinary way in a pot under glass. The variegated tradescantia is a very choice trailer, but a little more tender than the other, and requires a sunny position, while the plain green variety will do anywhere outside in the summer, even growing well under trees.

For autumn there are the hardy chrysanthemums, and if dwarf varieties with fibrous roots are chosen, a very good show can be made with these till the middle or end of November. The protection afforded them by the house keeps them in good condition longer than when they are in the open, especially when a thin veiling, such as tiffany, is afforded them on cold nights. Even newspapers will keep out several degrees of frost, and form a very cheap method of protection.

CHAPTER 15

Table Decoration and Flowers in Season

Graceful arrangement ~ How to manage thick-skinned stems ~ Colour schemes ~ Bad colours for artificial light ~ Preserving and resuscitating ~ Table of flowers in season.

The fashion of decorating tables to the extent now done is of comparatively recent date. When the duties were taken off the importation of foreign flowers, they became so much lower in price that the great middle class could afford to buy some even in midwinter. In the British Isles themselves, too, the carriage of flowers is much cheaper and more expeditious, though there is plenty of room for improvement still in that respect. The manner of arranging them has much altered, for, instead of cramming a clumsy vase to its utmost limits with a dozen different flowers of as many shades, only one, two, or at most three, kinds are now used, and these are set out in as graceful and airy a manner as possible. Plain glass vases, as a rule, show the blossoms off best, though pale green or ruby occasionally looks very well. The water need not be changed every day in all cases; it depends on the flower; wallflowers, for instance, turn the water putrid very soon, while it keeps fresh much longer where roses are concerned. The vases should, however, be filled up once a day, as the stems suck up moisture rapidly. Hardwooded flower stalks should receive special attention, or they will droop directly.

Stem splitting

Lilac, when cut and placed in water will absorb no more moisture than a lead pencil, unless the stems are split up; this can be done either with a hammer or a knife or both. As many leaves as possible should be left on the stems, for when under water they largely help to make the blossoms last well; it is only where the stalks are nearly leafless that the splitting and peeling is necessary.

Maidenhair fern may be made to last much longer if the end of the black, wiry stem is hammered for about an inch up.

It must not be forgotten that cutting from a plant strengthens it, and induces it to continue sending up flower stalks. People often seem chary of cutting their roses with any length of stem, I suppose because it has leaves and shoots all the way up, but this is an error; they should be cut with about eight or ten inches of stalk; pansies and violas also look much more natural when a portion of the shoot is cut along with each blossom.

By Parcel Post

On hot summer days, when flowers are to be sent by post, they should be picked early in the morning, several hours before they are to be sent off, and placed in bowls of water; then, if they are packed close together in tin, wood, or even cardboard boxes, they will arrive quite fresh at their destination, where otherwise they would be hopelessly faded. When a box of flowers is received, the contents should be put in lukewarm water in a dim light for an hour or so; they can then be rearranged in the vases they are intended to occupy.

Blue – a daylight colour

Some colours respond to artificial light much better than others. Most shades of blue are not suitable for decorating dinner tables, because they turn almost brown, or at best a dull mauve. In choosing violets, therefore, for evening wear, it will be found that the blossoms which have thin, rather washed-out petals of the lightest purple will look best, the full blue not being nearly so effective. For luncheon, an arrangement of purple clematis in vases on the palest pink ground is lovely, but does not look quite so well by gaslight, though here again if the least velvety flowers are chosen for evening, a good effect can be obtained.

Yellow is a splendid evening colour, but must be bright, or it will look merely cream. A dining room panelled in light oak, adorned with yellow marguerites alone, is very pleasing to the eye. In the spring, laburnum makes a novel dressing for a dining table; care, however, must be exercised with this flower, as the pods are poisonous. Blue also looks well with brown in the daytime; larkspurs, forget-me-nots, plumbago, campanulas, nemophilla, etc., all look very well. We know how artistic blue porcelain is on oak shelves, and, if the flowers have a white eye or are veined with white, the effect is somewhat the same. Scarlet is a good gas or electric light colour, but it must be used judiciously, and as a rule only be mixed with white, just as the ladies at a regimental ball are generally only allowed to robe themselves in this pure shade.

Simplicity

Nowadays the decorations are rarely made so high that one cannot see the other side of the table. Though this arrangement might occasionally be useful in hiding the face of an enemy, on the whole it was found inconvenient; accordingly they have climbed down; the 'bazaar stall' fashion is also disappearing, and flat table centres are used instead, or none at all. Simplicity is the great cry now, and though of course it may be costly, a charming effect is obtained with fewer flowers than was formerly considered correct, and is moreover easily imitated by an artistic eye in less expensive blossoms.

Some of the flowers to be had in each respective season are enumerated below. It will be noticed that where plenty of outdoor blossoms are to be had, the hothouse varieties are omitted.

Table of natural and forced flowers for each month

January
Natural
Christmas rose, Yellow jasmine
Forced
Carnations, Eucharis,
Gardenias, Poinsettias, Tuberoses,
Late chrysanthemums, Roman hyacinths,
Odontoglossum (orchid), Tulips,
Violet, single and double,
Narcissus

February
Natural
Christmas roses, Yellow jasmine,
Daphne, Snowdrops
Forced
White lilac, Carnation, Hyacinths,
Tulips, Geraniums, Marguerites,
Cattleya (orchid), Camellias,
Roses, Dicentra, Narcissus

March
Natural
Violets, Early narcissus, Almond blossom,
Cowslips, Polyanthus
Forced
Freesias, Lily of the valley, Arums,
Narcissus, Mauve lilac, Anemones,
Lilium Harrisii 'longiflorum',
Roses, Azaleas

April
Natural
Daffodils, Wallflowers, Forget-me-not,
Tulips, Alyssum, Anemones, Doronicums
Forced
Sweet peas, Roses, Carnations, Arums,
Lilies of the valley, Alliums,
Acacia, Epacris

May

Natural

Laburnum, Poet's eye narcissus,
Doronicums, Trollius, Iris, Parrot tulips,
Lilies of the valley,
Syringa, Lilac, Ranunculus

Forced

Arums, Ixias, Gladiolus (scarlet and white)

June

Natural

Sweet peas, Roses, Pinks, Pyrethrums (single),
Larkspurs, Canterbury bells, Penstemons, Lilies,
Columbines, Flag iris and other iris

July

Natural

Clematis, Montbretias, St. John's Wort,
Campanulas, Poppies (to be picked in the bud),
Carnations, Cornflowers, Indian pinks,
Erigeron (like an early Michaelmas daisy),
Gladiolus

August

Natural

Clematis, Coreopsis, Gaillardias,
Snapdragons, Sunflowers, Gladiolus,
Dahlias, Roses, Carnations

September

Natural

Michaelmas daisies, Pinks,
Chrysanthemums, Lilies, Sunflowers,
Japanese anemones, Roses

Forced

Tuberoses, Cattleyas,
Eucharis, Gardenias

October

Natural

Michaelmas daisies, Chrysanthemums,
Physalis (or Cape gooseberry), Violets,
Single Marigolds

Forced

Salvias, Marguerites, Tuberoses, Eucharis,
Odontoglossum, Cattleya, Bouvardia,
Roses, Carnations

November

Natural

Michaelmas daisies, Chrysanthemums,
The gladwin iris (berries), Violets

Forced

Eucharis, Geraniums, Marguerites,
Salvias, Carnations, Chrysanthemums,
Odontoglossum, Cattleya,
Bouvardia, Camellias

December

Natural

Yellow jasmine, Christmas roses

Forced

Salvias, Cypripediums, Violets,
Poinsettias, Geraniums, Chrysanthemums,
Lilies of the valley, Roman hyacinths,
Coelogyne (orchid),
Narcissus in variety

The cost of a flower is always in proportion to its blooming time. If lilies of the valley are wanted in August, they must be paid for heavily, as retarded bulbs (those which have been kept in ice) are used to produce them.

CHAPTER 16

The Propagation of Plants

By dividing ~ By cuttings ~ By seeds ~ By layers.

Propagation may be affected in various ways, of which division is perhaps the easiest. It must be done very carefully, or decay will set in. Some plants lend themselves to this form of propagation very readily; in others, the root stock is single and obviously resents division, wherefore it is better to try another plan. The Michaelmas daisies are good instances of the first kind; their roots are fibrous, and soon take to the new soil; it is tap-rooted plants which dislike division so much.

Careful division

It is advisable to divide most plants in the growing season, which is from spring to early autumn; if it is done in the winter months, each piece frequently remains quite inert and eventually rots. The plant should be taken up, with a fork by preference, and then pulled carefully apart with the hand. The smallest fragment of the old white anemone will grow, but few plants will stand quite so much division. Each piece should be well watered as it is planted, and if the sun is hot some shade improvised. Such things as delphiniums, phloxes, campanulas, and quick-growing subjects in general, should not be left too long without being divided, or the flowers will dwindle, and the plants become straggling in habit.

A good many plants which might be propagated by division of the roots are propagated instead by cuttings, as the flowers come finer in every way, and of course this method suits many plants which cannot be divided. Chrysanthemums present few difficulties; though the ultimate growth of this Japanese plant entails a vast amount of labour (if prizes are the object in view), yet cuttings from them are the easiest things possible to strike, even easier than a geranium, as there is no damping off. Cuttings are generally struck under glass, this method being the surest, even with hardy plants. The shoots selected should be well ripened, and the cut made squarely below a joint and be taken with a 'heel' if possible, that is, with a piece of the old wood attached. All but the topmost leaves should be pinched off, and then the cuttings must be inserted round the sides of the pot, and the soil well pressed down – the best cuttings in the world cannot make roots unless this be attended to. After that a good watering should be given them, and the pots set in a shady place till they have emitted roots, which may be known by the fact of their beginning to make new leaves. Some cuttings root better when the cut is allowed to form a 'callus', which in warm weather only takes a few hours.

Rose cuttings root very well out of doors on a north border, and trees produced in this manner are often very satisfactory, but they take a long while to come to a flowering stage, somewhat trying the patience of ardent amateurs.

One can gradually get quite a nice collection of interesting plants, by striking all the likely shoots in the different bunches of flowers received from friends, but it is generally best to identify them as soon as possible, so as to give each the right treatment.

Propagation by seed is quite a fascinating employment, and is a successful method, if pains are taken; though so many amateurs seem to fail. I have found it the safest plan, with all except the largest seeds, to bring them up under glass. Even the hardiest can be treated in this way, and one feels so much more sure of the result. For one thing, birds cannot get at them, therefore there is no need to make a network of black cotton to keep them off; neither can the cat meddle with them, and we all know pussy is a very bad gardener.

The pans specially sold for the purpose are the best, but pots will do very well. Fill them with fine moist soil, and press firmly down; then scatter the seed thinly on the top, and only cover with a slight layer of soil, afterwards placing in a dark corner. Where the seed is very small, do not cover with any mould at all, but, as an extra protection, place a piece of cardboard over the top of the pot, so that they shall not be blown away. Seeds like a still atmosphere, moisture, warmth, and darkness. Seeds and seedlings must not be watered in the ordinary way, but the pan containing them should be placed in a saucer of water, when enough moisture will be drawn up by capillary attraction. Thinning is extremely necessary; every plant must be given room to attain its full dimensions; where this is not done, the result is most unsatisfactory. As regards the time for sowing, of course, spring is the most usual, but in the case of annuals it will often be found a good plan to sow a few in autumn, as, by pursuing this method, nice stocky little plants are ready for the garden quite early in the season, and give flowers long before spring-sown seed could possibly do so.

Propagation by layering is very useful, as cuttings of some plants will not strike readily. Strong shoots are denuded of their leaves for a few inches, and their stems slit up and pressed into the ground by means of a peg; when firmly rooted, they can be detached from the parent plant by means of a pen knife. Carnations are generally reproduced in this way, as it is the surest method of all.

CHAPTER 17

The Management of Room Plants

Best kinds for 'roughing' it ~ Importance of cleanliness ~ The proper way of watering them.

The majority of English women like to see their rooms, and specially their drawing rooms, adorned with growing plants.

Nevertheless, a great many do not cultivate them successfully, so a few hints will not be amiss. Constant attention is needed to keep plants in perfect health, and this is exactly what is so often denied them. A lady buys two or three ferns that take her fancy, and feels for a while quite interested in their welfare; but, after a week or so, she leaves them to take care of themselves, which means to dwindle, and ultimately die. Many shillings, therefore, are constantly being spent in renewing plants which, with proper care, should last for years.

All room plants must be looked after daily, a few minutes every morning being far better than an hour once a week, which is all they receive in some homes.

I will treat first off palms, which, though such slow-growing subjects, seem the favourite of all for home decoration, owing to their grace of form and good lasting properties. If you observe the roots of most palms, you will see that, attached in an odd way to the rising stem is a sort of bulb, not unlike a pigmy potato. This excrescence, which should only be covered by a thin layer of soil, stores up nutriment for the plant's use, in much the same way as a hyacinth or daffodil does. This accounts in a great measure for its power in enduring dryness of the soil without flagging, which property, however, should not be abused. Palms should be watered as regularly, though not so often, as more sappy plants.

The correct way to water

Numbers of people do not know how to give water in the correct way, whereby the florist prospers! The golden rule is never to water a plant until it requires it, and then to do it thoroughly. It is fatal merely to moisten the top of the soil, and to leave the deeper roots dry. First give a sharp tap to the pot; if it rings, water is required; if, on the contrary, a dull sound is given out, the soil is wet enough. Lifting a pot is a sure test too, as one's hand soon becomes accustomed to the difference in weight of a moist and dry pot; the former, of course, being so much heavier. Always see that the water runs through the hole at the bottom of the pot, then you may be sure that each particle of soil is wet, and not till then. If you possibly can, it is best to use water of a corresponding temperature to that of the room they are in; this is most important with delicate plants. Large, shiny, horizontal-leaved plants require a weekly sponging to remove the inevitable dust which settles on them. Gloves should be worn while this is being done, as contact with the skin turns the edges of the leaves yellow; also gloves, of course, help to keep the hands soft and white. Plants with large leaves should never be watered overhead, unless immediately wiped dry, as each drop allowed to stand on the leaf turns yellow, rots, and finally quite spoils the leaf, so that it has to be removed. Palms will stand gas fairly well, but not so well as aspidistras.

The best plants for dark corners

An aspidistra (please note spelling) is the best plant there is for roughing it. The long, thick, dark leaves seem to stand draughts, gas, dark corners, poor soil, and general neglect almost with impunity. But here again watering overhead is fatal, as regards the appearance of these plants.

The leaves should be washed once a week, but I will just say here that where one is in a hurry, and cannot wait to get a sponge and water, a good polish with a duster is not at all a bad substitute.

There are disputes occasionally as to whether aspidistras ever flower. Of course, it is an undoubted fact that they do, and I can give a decided affirmative to any who may question it. My plants flower regularly every spring, but, as these blooms are a dull, greenish-purple in colour, and only sit, as it were, on the top of the soil, they are naturally overlooked.

The modesty of the violet is nowhere when compared with the aspidistra!

Aralias are good room plants, for they have a bold and handsome form, and glossy, bright green foliage, very like that of a fig. They do not stand gas well, however, but, as so many houses are lighted by electricity, this is less of a drawback than was formerly the case. If not regularly watered, too, they have a habit of dropping their leaves; otherwise they are of easy culture. As they grow taller, the lower leaves, even on a healthy plant, generally drop off.

Leggy plants

It is a good way, when these and kindred plants become 'leggy', to improve their appearance by cutting off the old root, and making them root higher up the stem. Where the plant is valuable, it is best to be sure of new roots before throwing away the old, but, as a rule, aralias have so many joints that they may easily be induced to strike by just pressing the stem firmly into the soil, then putting the pot in some dark place, and keeping the soil rather dry, though the foliage must be kept moist. To be quite sure of success, however, it is best to treat them in the following manner: Choose a handful of soil with a little loam in it, and, wetting the stem slightly, press the soil round two or three of the joints, and bind closely with some raffia or bass, being very careful to keep the soil always moist, or the plant will fail to make roots. Some people enclose this part of the stem in two halves of a small flowerpot, which is a good plan, if the stem will bear the weight, as it preserves a more even temperature.

The hare's-foot fern – Davallia canariensis – with its beautiful blue-green fronds, much divided and elegantly arched, makes the loveliest room plant imaginable, and, though fairly common, is not often seen in a good state of health. I have found that, on first buying a pot of this fern, the leaves almost invariably turn rusty and drop off, so that, as the new fronds sometimes do not appear for some while, an amateur might really be pardoned for imagining the plant dead. This is not so; the hare's-foot merely resents the change of atmosphere (it has probably been in a moist greenhouse), and, like most of us, takes time to settle down. Once it has acclimatised itself, there is no better plant to be had for the purpose. It is so essentially decorative that no one can fail to admire it. Firm potting is important in growing the davallia, and it does not seem so partial to water as most of the fern tribe. It will also stand gas pretty well, if not shut up for the night in an atmosphere charged with it, and this is the case with many room plants; they strongly object to being left to spend the night in the impure air, though a few hours each evening will not do them much harm. The plan of taking them out at bedtime also prevents so much dust accumulating on their leaves, an inevitable drawback where a room is thoroughly swept and dusted.

Always endeavour to keep your plants well balanced. In a room, it is impossible to do this, without constantly turning the pots round, so that all parts may get the light. In summer, this has to be attended to nearly every day, but in winter less often, as the sun is, of course, much less powerful.

As regards repotting, great care must be exercised, or more harm than good will result. Palms will grow for years in quite small pots, and do not thrive if over-potted. On the other hand, some plants require it annually, but, seldom or often, unless for some special reason, repotting should always be done in the spring. From the beginning of February until the end of May, a plant may safely be shifted on, as it is called, because all these months comprise the growing season, when fresh roots are emitted and new leaves being produced almost daily. See that the pot is perfectly clean and dry, and the soil in a friable condition; it should be composed of peat, loam and sand in equal parts; a little leaf mould, where it is for a fern proper, will be beneficial. A potting soil ready prepared may be had for about a shilling a peck from any seedsman, which saves time and trouble in mixing. Be sure to put clean crocks in at the bottom, or the soil will become sour. Shake the pot every now and again as you fill it up, to ensure no crevices being left; loose potting has caused the death of many a fine plant. When the pot is full, press the mould down, leaving from half an inch to an inch (according to the size) bare of soil to the rim of the pot, to allow of watering. It is well to put a layer, about half an inch thick, of cocoanut fibre on the top of the soil, as this looks neat, and serves to show off the foliage to the best advantage. Enough of the fibre to cover several dozen pots may be had for threepence. Guano is good, if supplied to the plants during the warmer months of the year. The proportions of guano to water can always be seen on the label pasted on the outside of the tin. It is well to remember that guano should never be given to a plant when the soil is dry, but always just after it has been watered.

Saucers or jardinieres should be emptied as a rule an hour after the plants have been watered, though where ferns seem to flourish most when allowed to stand in water, it is well to continue the practice. In very hot weather, this is undoubtedly of benefit to many plants, but in the winter the soil of all pot plants should err on the dry side, cold and damp together often proving fatal.

Good for two thirds of the year

There are some first rate plants which refuse to look well for the coldest part of the year (unless one is possessed of an hothouse), but which are really capital for brightening our rooms for at least eight months in the twelve. Of these, the asparagus 'fern' is perhaps the most useful. It is a lovely and graceful plant, which bears cutting, and it lasts so long, both in and out of water. Being, however, in reality a stove plant, amateurs who have no warmed greenhouse must not expect to keep it in thoroughly good health during the winter, but so soon as the spring appears, new green stems will shoot up in all directions, and the old fronds will soon be replaced by bright green feathery plumes of infinite grace.

Pteris wimsetti is a charming room plant.

Young eucalyptus plants are also very pretty for decorating a room, and are supposed to be good as a disinfectant. Their habit of growth is uncommon, and very charming to watch, as they quickly reach to an effective size, and make large handsome plants to set in the corners of reception rooms. It is best to bring them up by seed, which should be sown in February or March. Spring is the best time to buy room plants.

CHAPTER 18

Various Hints

Artificial manures ~ Labelling ~ Cutting off dead flowers ~ Buying plants ~ Tidiness in the garden, etc.

With far the larger half of our population the question of cost comes into everything. There are so many claims on our purses, that the money spent on recreations can only be a small part; moreover, is always liable to be drawn on at any moment. Somehow, the money laid out on a garden always seems to be grudged, especially when it is for such things as manure, so that if that item can be reduced, so much the better.

A 'wrinkle'

One good way of buying it, is to get the boys who sweep the roads to bring the contents of their cart to your garden instead of taking it away. Quite a lot can be purchased for sixpence or so, and the mixture is even more beneficial to some plants than the loads bought from the contractor. When the neat little heaps are swept up at the roadside, anyone may take it away. Householders can employ their own errand boys to do so, no charge being made whatever.

Guano and artificial manures in general are very stimulating, and must only be given to plants in bud, or at all events full growth. Sickly plants or those at rest must never have it. Soapsuds form a mild stimulant for rose trees in summer, but these things do not come in place of the manure with which the soil must be dressed in autumn; they are only additions.

Labelling

There has been much controversy over the labelling of plants; it must be done very delicately, or the appearance of the garden is spoilt; the word label usually presupposes a name to be written thereon, but, in reality, just a mark to show where a plant is, often seems all that is necessary, and this is very important indeed with plants which die right down every winter. The most unobtrusive tallies must be used, and they should be of zinc, or they will inevitably get lost. The wooden ones are all right in the greenhouse, but no good at all outside. For rose trees, names are required, and the 'acme' labels are much the best ever invented for these, and have now been in use by all rosarians for years; they can be had at Cant's Rose Nurseries, Colchester, for about 1 shilling 3 pence a dozen, post paid.

If we would keep plants in good health, all dead flowers must be cut off regularly; this is specially important in the case of sweet peas, pansies, and other free-flowering plants, which become poor, and soon leave off blossoming altogether, if allowed to form seedpods. It is a good plan to go round every morning with a basket and scissors, and snip off all faded blooms, as, when several days elapse, the work becomes long and irksome.

As regards buying plants, this comes somewhat expensive, until a little knowledge and experience has been gained. After a while, the different plants are known by sight, and one is able to see directly whether a flower or shrub is well grown and of good colour. Then, instead of ordering everything at the large nurseries, one can often pick up, in one's wanderings, very good things at small cost. Until that is the case, it is wiser to order from some reliable firm who is sure to send out everything true to name. People who go in for gardening, should always be ready to learn; there are so many points which cannot be acquired all at once. One can often gain a 'wrinkle' if one keeps one's eyes open, as the saying is. Constant visits should be made to Kew, Hampton Court, or any other well-kept public garden, if at all within reach. A stroll round a neighbour's garden, too, will often give one new ideas, and the interchange of opinions does a deal of good. A magazine keeps up one's interest wonderfully, and there are many specially published for amateurs. One must not be surprised that the advice often seems contradictory. The right way of growing a plant is the way that succeeds, and experience shows how varied may be the means by which success is attained. I should like here to warn my readers that before launching out into any great expense, they first come to a full understanding as to what they will or will not be able to take away. Greenhouses can be put up as tenants' fixtures, but a very slight difference in the manner of placing them may result in a good deal of unpleasantness with the landlord, and it is the same with rose trees, and other shrubs and plants. Where a shrub has attained to goodly proportions, it is really the best way to let it remain, even though the associations connected with it may be pleasant, as transplanting would probably mean death, in which case neither party would have gained anything. Of course, in the nature of things, a lover of gardening is loth to move at all, a rolling stone is not at all in his line.

Tidiness is most important in a small garden, especially in the winter time; plants may be allowed to get rampant in summer, but in the cold weather, this wildness tends to make it look miserable. One sometimes sees the brown, mildewed stalks of sunflowers and other tall plants, left on right into December, even in a front garden, and it gives such a deserted look to the place, that one longs to 'have at them' there and then with a knife. It is the same way with autumn leaves; in woods they look beautiful, as they flutter down and make a rich, rustling carpet for our feet, but, somehow, in the garden the beauty seems gone, and it is generally the best plan to sweep them away as soon as possible into some corner, where they can be left to turn into leaf mould. Of course there is a certain beautiful freedom which is very desirable in a garden, and which no one could call untidiness. What looks lovelier, for instance, than the jasmine, with its long sprays hanging down over the window, or the break made in a straight-edged path by some luxurious patch of thrift or forget-me-not? these are only fascinating irregularities!

Winter need not be a time for idleness; it must be spent in getting ready for the spring. Tools should be overhauled thoroughly, and new supplies of sticks and labels prepared. Plans, too, should be made for filling each different bed, so that when the warm days arrive, and one scarcely knows what to be at first, everything may be in train.

The faculty of looking ahead must needs be used, if we wish to succeed. I often think that living in anticipation constitutes a great part of the charm of gardening. When sowing the seed, have we not bright visions of the time when that selfsame seed will bear most exquisite blossoms? When pruning our rose trees, dreams of what they will become lend added interest to our occupations, and, indeed, this quality of imagination turns arduous work into a veritable labour of love, so that its devotees always aver it is the most delightful recreation in the world.

January
Average Temperature 37°

- In frosty weather wheel manure on to ground.
- See that every plant which is not quite hardy is well protected from frost.
- Shake off any snow which may be lying on the branches of fir trees, etc.
- In mild weather digging may be done.
- If it has not already been done, cut back all deciduous trees, such as chestnuts, limes and sycamores.
- Prune all except the tender fruit trees, cutting back weak shoots hard, and strong ones little.
- Sow early peas on a warm border.
- Do not transplant this month.
- Start covering rhubarb with pots or boxes for forcing, and surround them with manure.
- Paths may be relaid with gravel.
- The erection of arches, trellis work, or any alteration of this sort may be attended to.
- Keep all plants under glass clear of decaying leaves and anything likely to cause mouldiness.
- Raise temperature of greenhouses as the days become lighter.

February
Average Temperature 39°

- Begin sowing hardy annuals outside in a sheltered position.
- Refrain from pruning rose trees, or they will suffer later on.
- New lawns can be made now, though autumn is the best time.
- See that all trees are securely staked and shoots of wall climbers well nailed in before the winds of March come.
- Prune remaining fruit trees.
- Seeds of broad beans, peas, carrots, onions, beetroot, parsley, lettuce, etc., can now be sown, though the largest sowing should be made next month.
- Plants under glass must have more air and more water as they begin to grow quickly.
- Ventilate carefully and close all the houses before sunset.
- Give manure to fruit trees.
- Look over fuchsias, dahlias, etc.; cut back and place in gentle warmth.

March
Average Temperature 41°

- Hardy perennials may be planted.
- Prune hardy rose trees.
- Sow the bulk of flowering annuals.
- Cut back ivy during last week.
- Free the lawn of plantains and sow grass seed on bare patches.
- Renew or fill up box edgings.
- Hoe beds and borders frequently to keep down weeds.
- Rose trees may be planted, though autumn is the best time.
- See that bedding plants in frames have plenty of water.
- Clear out all dead plants and give a general tidy-up to the greenhouse.
- Give plenty of air from top lights to glasshouses.
- Plant out Jerusalem artichokes.
- Sow seeds of vegetables of all kinds.
- Pick up gravel paths, and give another layer if necessary.
- Protect anything newly planted from rough winds.
- Mulch bush fruit trees.

April
Average Temperature 46°

- Make last sowing of annuals and thin out those appearing above ground.
- Fill up gaps in the flower border.
- Plant out dahlias.
- Prune tea roses during first week.
- If rather dry weather ensues keep rockery and all spring-flowering plants well watered.
- Beds must be prepared for the tender plants put out next month by turning the soil well over and thus pulverizing it.
- Protect tender fruit trees from late frosts.
- Sow seeds of vegetables for succession.
- If the weather is hot, shading can be put on greenhouses.
- Bedding plants must be gradually hardened off by giving plenty of air.
- Mow and roll lawn frequently.
- Plant out potato tubers.
- Edgings can be planted or filled up.

May
Average Temperature 53°

- Keep a sharp lookout for insects.
- Commence bedding out this month and continue all through, reserving tender things such as coleus till the last.
- Hoe well between annuals and keep them well watered.
- Carefully train the various climbers or they will grow into an inextricable mass.
- Fill vases and baskets.
- Clip evergreen hedges as this makes them break out at the bottom.
- Put some strawy manure between the rows of strawberries and keep well watered.
- Sow vegetable seeds for succession.
- Plant out gourds, marrows, etc.
- If the weather is hot keep everything well watered.
- Transplant violets to their cool summer quarters.
- Syringe frequently under glass.

June
Average Temperature 59°

- If the garden is not altogether dependent on bedding plants it ought to be looking its freshest and best.
- See that everything has enough water.
- Continue to thin out flowering annuals as they increase in size.
- Carefully stake larkspurs, carnations, etc.
- If the leaves of spring bulbs have turned quite yellow, cut them off, but not before.
- Give copious supplies of water to all wall plants as a slight shower of rain scarcely touches them.
- Give occasional doses of manure to rose trees, and pick off all faded flowers.
- Water rockeries.
- Stake runner beans.
- Sow late broccoli.
- Sow more lettuce.
- Water peaches, apricots, etc., copiously.
- Mulch all fruit trees.
- Protect cherries from birds.
- Draw earth up round potatoes.
- Water marrows well and often with liquid manure.
- Early this month plant out tomatoes on a south or west wall.

- Keep greenhouses well ventilated both day and night.
- Harden off azaleas before being set outside next month.
- Most plants under glass will want watering twice a day or they must stand in a saucer of water.

July
Average Temperature 62°

- Look out for rose suckers and cut them off.
- Syringe rose trees.
- Mulch those going out of flower to induce them to make fresh buds.
- Keep faded flowers picked off.
- Commence propagating carnations.
- Take note of gaps in the flower beds and fill up from the nursery garden.
- Place azaleas, heaths, etc., outside in a shady place to rest awhile.
- Pansies which are blooming well on cool borders should have weak solutions of guano water afforded them.
- Cut down faded spikes of larkspur and mulch and water well.
- This month bedding plants are valuable as July is not a good month for herbaceous perennials.

- Stake the later runner beans.
- Plant out celery.
- Sow more turnip seed.
- Syringe both wall fruit and standards.
- Make new plantations of strawberries.
- Water lawn every day if possible.
- Thin out the superfluous wood of fig trees and shorten gross shoots on all fruit trees.
- Keep everything well watered under glass.
- Give air all night to greenhouses.
- Tie up climbers to roof neatly and frequently syringe.
- Damp down several times daily.

August
Average Temperature 61°

- Take pansy cuttings.
- Stake dahlias, phloxes, etc.
- Keep soil from caking by constant hoeing.
- Take cuttings of geraniums, fuchsias, etc., and strike them out of doors.
- Give copious supplies of water to rose trees and syringe foliage often.
- Cuttings of rose trees may be inserted now on a cool border.
- Rockeries must be constantly watered.

- Disentangle shoots of climbing plants and tie back artistically.
- Water lawn daily and do not cut too low.
- Cuttings of most plants may be taken now and inserted in a shady border with every chance of success.
- Cut down old raspberry canes to make way for the new.
- Protect fruit from wasps and other insects.
- Pinch off the tops of runner beans.
- Earth up celery and put out more young plants.
- Remove leaves which obstruct light on wall-peaches, apricots, etc.
- Syringe frequently.
- Give air day and night to greenhouses.
- Give constant supplies of liquid manure to chrysanthemums.
- Cut back climbing plants on the roof.

September
Average Temperature 57°

- Begin planting spring bulbs.
- Continue to take cuttings of bedding plants, but insert in frames now.
- Leave off giving outside plants stimulants.
- Sow hardy annuals to flower next Spring.

- Plant out rooted layers of carnations.
- Thin dahlia shoots and give plenty of water.
- Remove rose suckers.
- Pluck apples and pears as soon as ripe, and put on dry shelves to keep. The fruit should not touch.
- Prepare ground for new plantations.
- On hot days fruit trees can still be syringed to keep down insects.
- Plant out cabbages, sprouts, etc., from the seed bed.
- Earth up celery.
- Dig up and store potatoes.
- Towards the middle of the month remove greenhouse shading.
- Thin out climbers on roof again.
- Save for chrysanthemums guano is little needed now.
- Tender plants outside should be housed at the end of the month.
- Pot up fresias.
- Damp down less often and reduce the amount of air supplied.
- Ferns which were not repotted in the spring can be done now.

October
Average Temperature 50°

- Plant spring bulbs and the madonna lily.
- Take up all bedding plants and house carefully.
- Fill the beds with polyanthus, wallflower, forget-me-not and other early flowers.
- This is a good month for planting most things.
- Begin putting in shrubs.
- Thin out annuals sown last month.
- Cut back climbing plants.
- Keep hardy chrysanthemums well staked.
- Alterations can now proceed.
- Continue to pick pears and apples, and go over them daily to pick out mouldy ones.
- Commence planting fruit trees.
- Raspberry plantations should now be made.
- Mulch strawberry beds after forking lightly between the rows.
- Sow early peas in sheltered situations.
- Store potatoes, carrots, parsnips, etc.
- Give liquid manure to chrysanthemums under glass.
- Ventilate carefully and do not damp down.
- Bring September planted bulbs to the light as soon as they appear above ground.

November
Average Temperature 43°

- Plant rose trees.
- Mulch every rose tree in the garden.
- Continue planting hardy perennials.
- Cut down all dead stalks of dahlias, sunflowers, phloxes, etc.
- Finish planting bulbs.
- Roll lawn frequently. New ones can now be made.
- Continually tidy up the garden.
- Finish planting shrubs.
- Protect fig trees by mulching and cut back some of the over-luxuriant shoots.
- Plant fruit trees of all kinds.
- Trench ground not in use that the rain and frost may sweeten it.
- Prune currants and gooseberries.
- Hoe frequently between rows of cauliflower and cabbage.
- Celery must be earthed up higher.
- Any alterations that may be in hand should be completed this month.
- See that oil lamp and other heating apparatus is in good order.
- Look over cuttings of geraniums, etc., and remove all decayed leaves, which should be burnt.
- Ventilate all glass houses much less, especially during fogs.

December
Average Temperature 39°

- Give a final glance to tender plants to see that they are well protected.
- Cut down faded stalks of hardy chrysanthemums.
- Place hand lights over Christmas roses.
- This is a good time for writing new labels, preparing stakes, and making plans for the following summer.
- Roll gravel walks, and if mossy sprinkle with salt.
- Planting of fruit trees may continue if the weather be mild.
- Thin out gross wood to allow the air to circulate.
- Wheel manure on to the ground in frosty weather.
- Prepare vegetable seeds for sowing, by separating them from the husk, drying, labelling and sorting them.
- Earth up greens of all kinds with the hoe.
- In glasshouses avoid too much moisture at this dead season of the year.
- Only ventilate in mild, calm weather.
- Keep everything scrupulously clean.
- Give as much light as possible to growing things.
- Plants at rest should be kept dark.

Terms used by gardeners

Mulching – Term used for applying manure in a thick layer round the roots of shrubs, as a protection from frost.

Pricking off – Transplanting seedlings into separate pots.

'Eyes' – Incipient leaf buds.

'Heel' – The hardened part of a cutting, formed where it is joined to the original plant.

Annual – Lasting one year.

Biennial – Lasting two years.

Perennial – Lasting several years.

Herbaceous – Term applied to plants which die down completely every winter.

Deciduous – Not evergreen; this term is applied to trees the leaves of which fall off every autumn.

Suckers – Shoots that spring up from the common stock, as distinct from those which belong to the engrafted portion.

Pegging down – Bending branches down close to the ground, and securing them with a peg.

Runners – Separate little plants, issuing from the parent, and ultimately rooting for themselves.

Spit – A spade's depth.

'Strike' – A term applied to cuttings making roots.

Pinching out – Rubbing off undesirable shoots.

'Blind' – A term applied to plants which turn out flowerless.

Heeling in – The process of temporarily covering plants with soil, till the weather is suitable for setting them out in their permanent quarters.

Carpet bedding – The geometrical arrangement of plants.

www.ingramcontent.com/pod-product-compliance
Lightning Source LLC
Chambersburg PA
CBHW032040290426
44110CB00012B/892